needfinding

design research and planning

fourth edition

Dev Patnaik

Needfinding: Design Research and Planning

Contents

Introduction

Needfinding was originally developed at Stanford University as a means to help designers get closer to end users. Exploration of these methods was first begun in the 1960s by Robert McKim, then the head of Stanford's Product Design Program.

McKim noticed that the leaders in any organization were those people who found important new problems to work on, not necessarily those who ultimately solved the problems. The greatest impact that designers could have on product development, then, was at the earliest stages of product definition. As a response, he began synthesizing an approach to studying people to identify their unmet needs. He termed that approach Needfinding.

Needfinding is the act of discovering people's explicit and implicit needs so that designers can create appropriate solutions.

The term Needfinding is a bit of a historical artifact. After all, Needfinding is about more than just needs. On the way to identifying needs, designers learn all sorts of important contextual information about the world. This includes insights about activities that people do, and frames for how they think. As such, Needfinding incorporates what can generally be called design research.

Needfinding is also about more than just finding. Over the years, Needfinding's practitioners have sought to make their insights more and more useful for practicing designers. As a result, Needfinding has come to include elements of design planning: providing guidance and strategies for what a successful solution might be.

Needfinding has thus evolved into a methodology that's a hybrid of both design research and design planning. That hybridity is one of Needfinding's core strengths.

Many designers struggle to characterize the needs of users who don't yet exist. Traditionally, companies have used market research methods such as surveys and focus groups to get information about people. These methods work well in quantifying customers' preferences among existing solution options, but they do little to identify those needs that people can't readily articulate.

To acquire more qualitative information on customers, many companies have used research methods drawn from sociology and anthropology. These social research methods result in a rich description of people's behavior, interactions, and environmental conditions. However, such methods in and of themselves don't focus on the user needs and consequent business opportunities that customers present. Research can often be more descriptive than prescriptive. For the full potential of qualitative research to be harnessed, it must be better integrated into the process of design and development. It has to link the activities of marketing and design professionals alike.

Why focus on needs?

Most designers intuitively understand that needs are important. They know that they do their best work solving people's problems when they clearly understand what those problems are. However, an understanding of people's needs can be leveraged across an entire business activity, providing value beyond the development of any single product. The points below examine how a research effort focused on needs can

help companies plan both short and long-term product development and allow design managers to determine which problems to solve first.

Needs last longer than any specific solution.

Solutions come in and out of favor faster than the needs they serve. Punch cards, magnetic tape, and 5¼" floppy disks have successively moved from introduction to obsolescence. However, the underlying need to store computer data has existed throughout the lives of each of those products and continues to exist today. Because needs endure longer than solutions, companies should focus on satisfying those needs rather than on just maintaining an existing offering.

Thinking of the company as a provider of a solution may encourage the company to continue improving that solution, but it rules out creating entirely new offerings that satisfy the need in different ways. Conversely, focusing on needs encourages companies to continue innovating better ways to serve those needs, independent of current solutions.

Needs aren't guesses at the future. They're existing opportunities waiting to be unlocked.

Strategy and product development need not depend solely on predicting the

Needfinding: Design Research and Planning

future. A crucial part of that future already exists today. While solutions that eliminate needs do occasionally appear, the problems that currently trouble people are likely to continue into the future. Working to solve them is less risky than creating a plan around a prophecy of what tomorrow holds.

Although there's no promise that a particular solution is the correct one, focusing on needs can at least assure companies that they are working on problems that will still exist in an undisclosed future. By understanding people's needs, companies can better gauge whether consumers will be interested in a new product.

Needs provide a roadmap for development.

People's needs give companies a method for determining what corporate skills and new offerings should be developed to grow their businesses. A company currently may not have the capabilities necessary to satisfy all of a customer's needs. But by identifying the needs that cannot currently be satisfied and then working toward meeting them, the company charts a development path to guide its efforts. Back in the days of old days of film photography, Eastman Kodak realized from studying customers that people didn't just want film and photo processing. Rather, they looked to Kodak to serve their need to capture and enjoy images of daily life. Kodak developed a roadmap to better satisfy that need, gradually advancing the company into previously unknown areas such as Photo CDs and image manipulation software. When Kodak initiated this roadmap, it knew relatively little about creating imaging software for home computers. Yet, because such knowledge was crucial to serving the long-term needs of its customers, the company developed its capabilities over time.

Needs inspire action.

Without emphasizing needs, qualitative social research creates a vivid picture of the customer's experience without prescribing ways to improve it. Even the most detailed description of customers' behavior and environments is of limited value to product developers if it doesn't include actionable imperatives to guide their work. Needs provide this impetus for action. Once a need has been identified, designers understand the problem to be solved.

Needs are obvious after the fact, not before.

People become acclimated to their problems, often developing work-arounds to circumvent the underlying needs. In doing so, they can become oblivious to the needs' existence. A well-conducted research effort that doesn't merely rely on the customer to describe his situation can uncover these latent needs. Because many needs are apparent only after they've been solved, research focused on needs suggests opportunities that competitors may not be considering. Bajaj Auto, based in India, is the world's largest motor-scooter manufacturer. For decades, most Bajaj scooter owners would insist that they were happy with how the product operated. Yet before starting a Bajaj scooter, the rider would have to tilt it to fill the eccentrically mounted engine with fuel. Bajaj owners only recognized this problem after Honda introduced a model in India with a center-mounted engine that didn't require tilting.

Core Principles of Needfinding

Needs are important, but they're also difficult to see. Although previously undiscovered needs occasionally appear to designers out of happenstance, most of us aren't that lucky. Uncovering needs reliably requires an organized research effort. Needfinding gives designers and companies the tools necessary for illuminating needs and using them for product development. The following points characterize the philosophy behind Needfinding, providing guidelines for practitioners.

Look for needs, not solutions.

Looking for needs rather than specific solutions keeps all possible solutions

open for consideration, rather than prematurely limiting possibilities. Needfinding researchers state needs independently of how those needs might be served. For example, a store clerk might need to get some boxes from a high shelf. Instead of stating that the clerk needs a ladder, a Needfinding researcher would record that he needs access to boxes on the top shelf. The need leaves open possible solutions that range from using a forklift, to rearranging the boxes, to creating entirely new solutions.

Make research and design seamless.

Needfinding researchers are often designers trained in research methods or researchers taught how to conceptualize designs. They may approach the process from a traditional marketing background. In any case, these researchers are involved both in studying people and in conceptualizing new products. This approach allows for a seamless transition between research and design. The research is guided by the information necessary for product development, and the design work is conducted with a tacit understanding that could only be acquired by carrying out the research. Translation between the research and design stages of a project is greatly reduced, and both phases of the project are more effective knowing the requirements of the other phase.

Spend time in the participants' world.

Researchers obtain the richest information on people's needs by observing and interviewing customers first-hand. The researchers can then directly see many small but important details about the customer's activities and the context in which they occur, details that wouldn't be available outside of that context. By directly observing customers' activities, Needfinding avoids a reliance on customers' memory, descriptive ability, or awareness of a need. In addition, the customer's environment facilitates communication between the researcher and customer by allowing them to refer to and use objects in the environment during the discussion.

Look beyond the immediately solvable problem.

Researchers—especially designers conducting research—often don't see beyond problems that they can immediately solve. This impediment unnecessarily limits the information gathered. To gain the full value of conducting research, Needfinding asks researchers to record and analyze issues that may seem far beyond the scope of the immediate project. Recognizing and dissecting these deeper problems allows the company to plan for the issues that should be fixed down the road, even when those problems aren't currently solvable. A scooter manufacturer

discovered that customers were annoyed by how dirty their clothes got riding to work. While this couldn't be helped in their new scooter design, the problem was marked as an issue that could provide opportunities for long-term innovation.

Let the participants set the agenda.

Although researchers may go to the customer's environment knowing what kind of information is desired, it's important to give the customer leeway to guide activities and discussions. In Needfinding research, customers control the proceedings—at least to the extent that their activities and discussions relate to the research topic. This prevents researchers from prompting the customer on what to do next, and keeps the study open to serendipitous insights.

Collect eclectic forms of data.

Information about people comes in many forms. A facial expression might express a person's emotions better than her words. Keepsakes found in an office might reveal information about a person's relationship with his work. Needfinding researchers record all of these forms of data for later study away from the site, as analyzing data in the customer's environment distracts the researcher from collecting it. Researchers often pay special attention to contradictions between different sources of data, as these contradictions often point to previously unrecognized or unarticulated needs.

Make findings tangible and prescriptive.

Written descriptions alone often don't make the customer's needs real to those who haven't been involved in the research. To make decisions based on the research, the findings must be presented in a vivid and actionable form. The needs are better understood when supplemented with drawings, photos, audio recordings and/or video. Because Needfinding leads to design, researchers also recommend what might be done to satisfy the customer's requirements. Providing the results in a prescriptive, tangible form allows for a smoother transition between studying people's needs and creating new ways to meet them.

Iterate to refine the findings.

Needfinding uses many quick passes to study people, rather than a single, long research effort. This approach allows design work to proceed in parallel with the research. After each pass, the researchers offer a "draft" of the findings, outlining their current understanding of customers' needs and contexts. Preliminary design work can then begin, based on this early hypothesis. When more information is needed to complete a design, researchers return to the field for further study. As the researcher-designers gain a better understanding of

people's needs, they also refine the products created to serve those needs.

Collaborating Across Disciplines

Companies face constant pressure from competitors to improve their offering. This has pushed product development organizations to optimize their processes around incremental improvement. As the traditional link between a company and its customers, marketing professionals have asked end users to articulate opportunities for immediate improvement. Design and engineering has then been chartered to make these improvements real. This approach has had notable success in industries where linear improvements in performance – faster, smaller, cheaper, using less power, etc. – are most desired.

However, this approach breaks down when companies seek to completely rewrite a product's specifications or create something entirely new. While people can easily express their preferences among a set of known options, solutions that aren't immediately apparent can go unvoiced. Companies can find that their customers express a desire for an improvement only after a competitor has created it. This forces marketing into the reactive role of asking for things that the competition already has. Developers, in turn, are then working to a timeline that is, by definition, already too late. When

Needfinding: Design Research and Planning

linear improvements fail to provide a decisive advantage, new opportunities must be discovered in advance.

Needfinding offers designers a different dynamic for understanding customers, one that has a role for both marketers and designers. The methodology outlined here is a broad overview of how those involved in product development can preemptively discover opportunities for competitive advantage. Needfinding isn't the exclusive territory of any one discipline. Both marketers and designers need to work together to discover customers' needs. These needs, in turn, suggest areas of innovation for designers, as well as new markets that await development. The result is a dialog between company and customer, rather than between marketing and design. In this way, both groups can work together to create innovative new solutions, and leap past competitors devoted to incremental change.

The book you're now holding is intended to be an introduction to Needfinding methodology for the novice designer or design thinker. In actuality, it's really just a loose amalgamation of Needfinding methods. Reading it won't really teach you how to do Needfinding. Like so many aspects of design, Needfinding as a subject is less like History and more like Golf. You learn it by doing it. Treat this text like a reference guide to a subject that really exists in out in the world and in the actions you take.

This book is also a work in progress. Like in any healthy practice, new methods are constantly being developed and old ones fall out of favor. I hope that you find exceptions and callouts to what's presented. I hope you scribble in the margins and add in your own insights from the field. Most of all, I hope you give it a try. If you do, you may just find that Needfinding is a great approach, not only to make better things, but to make things better.

The Design Process

Needfinding is the act of discovering people's explicit and implicit needs so that you can create appropriate solutions. Often, these needs aren't so easy to find. Moreover, when we can find out a reasonable set of needs, we often have difficulty translating them into appropriate solutions. To both find important needs and develop them into compelling solutions, it's necessary to move beyond what we can tangibly sense into more abstract realms of concepts, frameworks and ideas.

Charles Owens at the Illinois Institute of Technology developed the following two by two matrix to describe the cyclical process that designers move through as they understand a situation, conceptualize a solution, express it, and test it. It includes four quadrants:

The Design Process
The act of creating a new design can be seen as a process whereby the designer toggles between the concrete world and abstract concepts, between analysis of the situation and synthesis of a desired result.

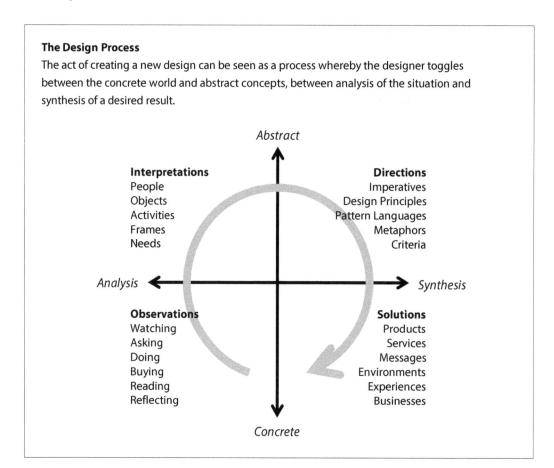

Observations.

Observation is about looking out into the world and into yourself to understand the situation and gather findings. See the world with fresh eyes. Listen & Learn. Find new points of view. There are six different ways that we can observe ourselves and others.

- *Watching*
- *Asking*
- *Doing*
- *Buying*
- *Reading*
- *Reflecting*

Interpretations.

Interpretations are about making sense of what you see and turning findings into insights. Notice patterns, uncover their underlying causes, and build models to explain what's going on. Typically, these patterns are described in the form of frameworks. There are five different kinds of data that we organize into frameworks to make interpretations, in order of increasing abstraction.

- *People*
- *Objects*
- *Activities*
- *Frames*
- *Needs*

Directions.

Creating directions is about turning insights into actions and determining appropriate approaches for design. Define what good looks like at varying levels of detail. There are five different kinds of directive information that we can create, in order of increasing concreteness and specificity.

- *Imperatives*
- *Design Principles*
- *Pattern Languages*
- *Metaphors*
- *Criteria*

Solutions.

The solutions phase of the process is about creating the tangible product, service or system to fill the need. It's about making concepts tangible so you can have an impact and get feedback. Doing this is really a whole book in itself, and we therefore can't cover all of it here. There are six different kinds of solutions that designers create.

- *Products*
- *Services*
- *Messages*
- *Environments*
- *Experiences*
- *Businesses*

Observations

Observation is about looking out into the world and into yourself to understand the situation and gather findings. See the world with fresh eyes. Listen & Learn. Find new points of view. There are six different ways that we can observe ourselves and others.

- Watching
- Asking
- Doing
- Buying
- Reading
- Reflecting

Intro to Observations

Observation is about seeing the world in new ways. As Marcel Proust said, "The real magic of discovery lies not in seeking new landscapes but in having new eyes." Acknowledge that you have your own personal way of seeing the world, and get ready to challenge it. We're all wired to intuit each other's' thoughts and feelings. But the pressures and cultures of today's business world can keep us from tapping into that skill.

Separate out what you see from what you interpret.

When it comes to observing others, try to turn off your inner interpretations. Don't assume you know why they do what they do — ask. When debriefing, articulate what you see, before launching into what you think it means. We will revisit our interpretations many times, but we should keep the facts as pure as possible.

Build rapport.

No one will tell you their deepest and most personal stories the second you meet them. Spend time learning about them and building a relationship so they will be comfortable when you get to topics that they may be reticent to talk about.

Record what you observe.

Observations that seem relatively unimportant in the moment can reveal important insights upon further reflection. Of course, that requires you to record what you see and hear for later analysis. Use recording media to capture the richness of information in the world so that it can be studied further later.

Taking Notes.

When documenting a discussion with a participant, record the person's statements in her own words as much as possible. The person's choice of words can carry meaning that would be lost if the researcher were to translate them.

That said, the participant may make statements that are too general to guide design work. In such cases, use follow-up questions to get to the desired level of detail, still recording the subsequent answers in the customer's words. Open-ended questions are especially useful for this purpose, as they give customers an opportunity to describe situations in their own words. In addition, it is often useful to have the customer interpret video recordings of their own activities, explaining the motivation for their actions in their own words.

Choosing a recording medium.

Video, audio, photos, and drawings each offer different advantages. Decide what kinds of information will be important to the study, reasonably easy to capture in participants' environments, and minimally intrusive to the customer's activities. Then proceed accordingly. Video allows you to later review real time processes in detail. Audio recording captures environmental sounds and exact wordings more inconspicuously than video. Photographs portray images of reality that can be easily categorized and sorted for comparisons. Drawings can capture details invisible to the eye such as obscured features and object cross sections.

Watching

The secret to observing is to **watch**, **get bored**, then **watch some more**. Giving yourself time allows you to get past your own filters.

Separate out what you **observe** from what you **interpret**. Sometimes your interpretations can lead you astray. Sometimes they can tip you off to what's really going on.

Note things that are interesting, notable or unexpected. Then spend time analyzing **why** you think they're special.

Watching: Figure & Ground

Painters originally developed the idea of focusing on the figure, or center of attention, versus the ground or surrounding context. In Western Culture, we tend to place a tremendous amount of importance on figures, and ignore much of the surrounding contextual information. That often leads us to be challenged by the sorts of illustrations shown below. For instance, in the picture below, are we looking at two people? Or a vase?

This concept is incredibly important when we start to observe the real world. While the world outside may not have literal black and white figure and ground arrangements to toggle between, it may have all sorts of valuable contextual information that we would otherwise ignore if we gave overwhelming emphasis to our "center of attention." When making observations, it's a good idea to determine your frame of observation:

What's in the frame?

What's out of the frame?

What's important?

What isn't important?

Watching: A.E.I.O.U.

One of the basic challenges of an observation exercise is simply recording all of the data. While video and audio recordings can help to capture a lot of what's going on, the resulting "raw" data still needs to be codified to get to the basic elements of the scene. Rick Robinson, the founder of E-Lab developed A.E.I.O.U. framework as a handy way to put the mass of observational data into some simple buckets. When you're out in the field, a good place to start your observations is by noting the following five elements.

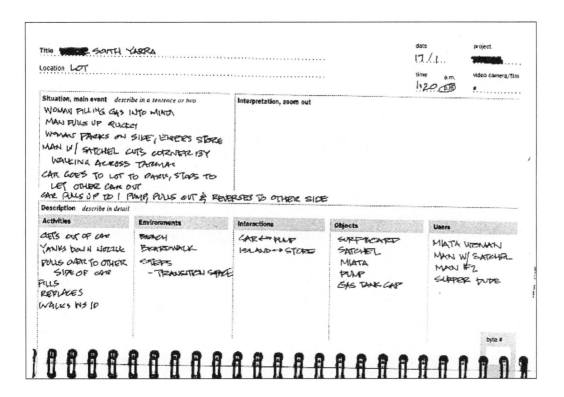

Activities

What are the actions and behaviors that you can observe taking place? These can be listed at multiple levels, from the overall objective-based description (i.e. filling the car up with gas) down to the minute activities (i.e. opening the gas cap cover, unscrewing the gas cap, placing the cap on top of the pump, etc.)

Environments

Describing the venues or overall setting that you're in can help to provide useful context. Note that this can include multiple environments, for instance when following a person along on a shopping trip.

Interactions

Record the basic interactions between the people you see, between people and objects, and even between objects. This is one category that may be more useful if it's linked to other factors such as a timeline.

Objects

What are all the objects that you see? This may include both natural objects and man-made artifacts. Use this list as a jumping off point to describe particular objects in greater detail. As a designer, you may start to see some basic patterns in what exists where and why. The entire discipline of material culture concerns itself with using descriptions of objects to interpret the values, behaviors and meaning structures of the people who use them.

Users

Finally, and often most importantly, who are the people that you see in your observation? People is, after all, a better word but, hey, it doesn't start with a U…Who are the people? What are their names? Their relevant job titles? The role they play in the community or social network? Is one a fireman? A sister? A bully?

Asking

Let your participants **set the agenda**. Follow their lead and you might learn things you didn't know that you didn't know.

Spend time **building rapport**. Always respect and acknowledge the responses you get.

Ask simple, **open-ended questions**. Avoid "leading the witness" or challenging their statements.

Listen 90%, talk 10%. This isn't a conversation; it's an interview. Limit talking about yourself.

Use the **participants' own words**. Never correct their words or pronunciation. Put them in the role of the expert.

Record what you see and hear. Record quotes **verbatim**.

Remember that for you, this is a class. For your participants, this is their lives. It's important to maintain your **respect** for them even as you maintain your **distance**!

Asking: Questions

Asking questions is the basic way in which we can find out what people are thinking. More importantly, our questions serve as prompts for people to tell us stories about their lives. Here are different types of questions you may want to use.

Starter Questions

Introduction. "Why don't you start by telling us a little about yourself…?" "What specifically do you do here?"

Sequence. "Walk me through a typical day…" "Then what do you do next?"

Specific Examples. "Let's take last night for example, what did you make for dinner?"

Detail and Overview Questions

Tasks and organizational structures. "Can you draw me a diagram of your computer network?

Exhaustive List. "What are all the different exercises you do in ballet class" "Are there any others?"

Quantity. "How many of your customers fall into that category?"

Investigative Questions

Suggestive Opinion. "Some people have really negative feelings about mobile phones while others don't at all. What are your feelings about them?"

Native Language. "Why do you call it the 'Batcave??"

Clarification. "…and when you say easy to use, you mean what?"

Empathic Questions

Participation. "Can you show me how I should make a Whopper?"

Naïve Outsider Perspective. "Let's say that I've just arrived here from another country, what can you tell me about the typical American breakfast?"

Questions to Spur Reflection

Changes Over Time. "How are things different than they were a year ago?"

Projection. "Do the other cashiers feel that way, or differently?"

The Why Question. Use with great care, "Why didn't you look both ways before crossing?"

Asking: Ethnographic Interviews

Ethnography is the rigorous study of the routine daily lives of a group of people. It was originally developed by empires to better understand their conquered subjects. Today, it has far more benign applications. More than anything, ethnography is about thick description – getting it all down.

An Ethnographic Interview

Ethnographic interviews are extended "open ended" interviews exploring the behaviors, context and meaning of an experience.

Specific techniques include making the interview feel like a conversation, alternating between different types of questions, moving from "outside" to "inside" (actions vs. thoughts), encouraging stories over short answers, gently guiding the interview towards topics relevant to your interests.

The general flow of an interview can often follow the flow of a good story.

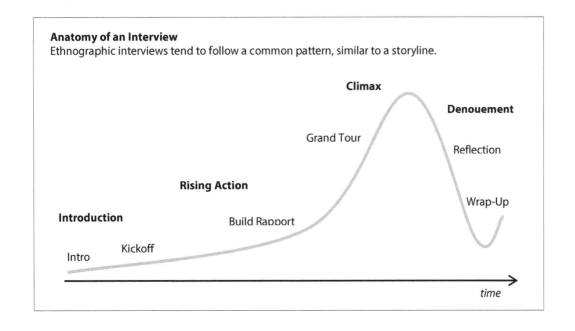

Anatomy of an Interview
Ethnographic interviews tend to follow a common pattern, similar to a storyline.

Climax

Denouement

Grand Tour

Reflection

Rising Action

Wrap-Up

Introduction

Build Rapport

Intro

Kickoff

time

Introduction and Kick Off.

Set up a comfortable place for the interview. Describe your purpose. Let them know their knowledge is important. Establish partnership between you and the participant.

Build Rapport.

Ease defensiveness through reassurance. Start with general concrete questions, and then explore their experiences. Let them tell the stories they want to. Build rapport through description of an average day of contacts. Choose a particularly interesting contact experiences.

Grand Tour,

Ask interviewee for a narrated tour of the setting. Ask questions, act out scenarios. Probe for details and emotional issues.

Reflection,

At end of interview explore more abstract feelings and thoughts. Repeat back what you heard to evoke further response. What are successes & failures around that contact? Get them to reflect upon challenges & contradictions.

Wrap-Up.

Expect important information after interview is officially "over."

Doing

Observe first, by watching, asking, or reading. Then try something out for yourself. This gives you context to the situation.

Observe not just the situation, but also **observe yourself** and your reactions. What did you see? What did you think? What did you feel?

Look for discrepancies between what people say—and believe—and what actually happens.

Get someone to be a **guide** through your experience. Be **safe**. Don't do anything that puts yourself in danger.

Buying

The benefit to buying is to **experience the whole journey** and understand the context surrounding a purchase. Continue to watch, ask, and do as you buy.

Observe the environment and yourself. Map out the **highs and lows** of your journey and the **decisions** you make.

Consider different paths that would lead someone to make a purchase and go through them yourself.

Buy around the things you're interested in. **Look for analogs**, direct and indirect competitors, and try them all out.

Reading

Prior to stepping out into the field to get primary data, **build on the work of others** and avoid reinventing the wheel.

Mine secondary sources such as literature, broadcast media and websites.

Go broad. Look for existing data as well as others' analysis, specific pieces of information as well as new questions, the state-of-the-art as well as untapped opportunities.

Use diverse sources like books, magazines, industry reports, prior research, case studies, websites, and blogs.

Strike a balance between general business and culture resources and project and industry specific ones.

Reading: Issues Mapping

Issues Maps are a helpful tool used to synthesize secondary research. Their goal is to identify connections between topics and hone in on critical areas that directly impact an industry or market. We can narrow down the set of issues of which the team needs to develop deeper understanding and show stakeholders that we're making conscious choices about where to focus, rather than leaving areas out by neglectful omission.

Guidelines for Creating Issues Maps

- *Note interesting stories, facts, and themes while reading secondary research.*
- *Visually link together related issues.*

- *Start the map with all the themes, not just the ones that are traditionally most important.*
- *Use a mix of text, visuals and call-outs*

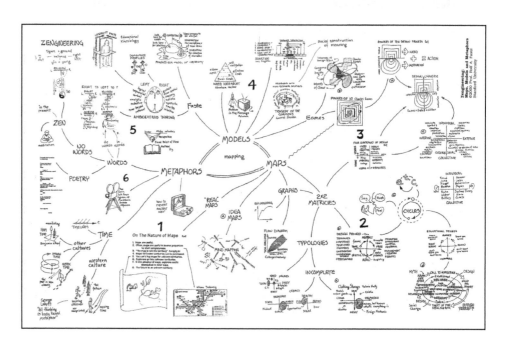

Reflecting

If you give yourself the **time and space** to reflect, you'll often discover that you know more than you think you do.

Use your **idea log** as a **thought partner**– a sounding board to capture ideas and show your thinking to yourself.

Use **mindmapping** to help you draw out what you experienced and put it on paper.

Use **powers of ten** to change the scale of your thinking up or down.

Ask **why** again and again to get to what's really going on.

Reflecting: Debriefing

The debrief offers an opportunity to engage with what you've seen and heard in the field while the experience is still fresh in your memory. Take advantage of this time as a team to share initial thoughts and make sense of what you've seen. Let surprises and questions come into the open. Trust your gut: things that strike you early on probably do so for a reason, so make sure to capture all that comes up in the discussion.

Getting the information out on the table early enables you to start making connections and begin your initial analysis. Below are some questions to ask yourself and your team while you are going through your research experience.

Initial Impressions.

What did you learn, right off the bat? What surprised you?

Their Motivations and Priorities.

What's important to them? What motivated or inspired them? What keeps them up at night?

Pain Points.

What pressure did they face? Where is change about to happen in their lives?

Social Connections and Roles.

What relationships are in their lives, and what are their roles?

Participant Profiles.

If your participants had a trading card outlining basic personal facts, what would it say?

What the Heck?

What was odd or unusual? What made no sense to you?

Activities and Tasks.

How did they perform particular tasks or processes? Did they do anything differently than we might have expected?

What Else?

What other things would you like to know?

Needfinding: Design Research and Planning

Reflecting: Idea Logs

Everyone has great ideas. Great ideators write them down. They maintain a log of their ideas—both the inspired and the absurd ones. Used most effectively, the log is not just a means of recording ideas; it also acts as a triggering device to help generate even more concepts. Random observations and half-baked thoughts recorded in the logs are used as inspiration for new, more promising ideas, or even pulled out months later when an ideator finds a suitable application.

The mere act of flipping through an idea log provokes new ideas, but this triggering mechanism can occur in a variety of other ways too. The spatial relationship of two seemingly disparate ideas on a page can stimulate new idea combinations and new ways of thinking about a problem.

Ideators who experience the most benefit from their logging also feed the outcomes of lessons they learn back into their logs, creating branches of inquiry that continue indefinitely.

The Origins of Logbooks

Historically a logbook was a journal a captain kept to record progress and the condition of his ship. It was a way to record the ship's speed and direction, meteorological conditions, and condition of the crew (including punishments and deaths). It was a compulsory document that was sent to the proper authorities after each voyage.

Captains who failed to keep an accurate log, or falsified entries after the event, were disciplined. And in those storied years, discipline was harsh.

The log itself was originally a large wooden board attached to a line knotted every 7 fathoms or so. At the change of every watch it would be tossed overboard at the same time as a 28 second sandglass was turned over. When this time "ran out" (note the source of this metaphor), the line was stopped. This gave a time and distance from which the ships speed could be calculated, or actually just read off in "knots". Today, a log is any device that measures a ship's speed.

A Designer's Logbook

A design logbook applies these ideas metaphorically, less the hanging that accompanied doing a poor job. A logbook need be nothing more than a record of the progress of your thinking.

A logbook isn't something that should need to be done after the fact to 'present' your thinking. Such journals are the bread and butter of any person involved in the development of ideas.

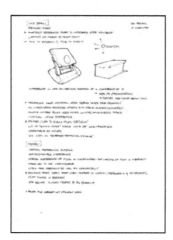

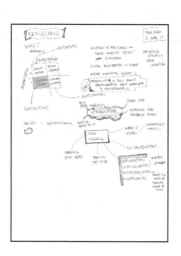

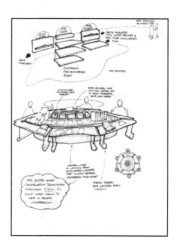

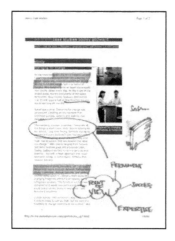

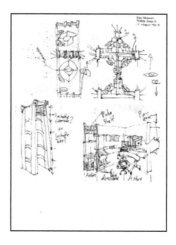

DaVinci's Logbooks

Leonardo DaVinci was one of the all-time greatest idea loggers. His explorations of natural and mechanical phenomenon covered many years and topics, as did his sketch-studies of anatomy and composition.

While each notebook entry may not have seemed significant at the time, DaVinci used these elements to develop major works and thorough observations. As Daniel Boorstin pointed out, his logbooks are now considered designs unto themselves.

"After his death the five thousand pages of his notes were widely dispersed as collectors' items. Nearly every page revealed the cosmic miscellany of his mind, the indiscriminate reach of his curiosity. A single page, for example, taking off from his interest in curves, shows an exercise in the geometry of curves, a drawing of curly hair, grasses curling around an arum lily, sketches of trees, curvesome clouds, rippling waves of water, a prancing horse, and the design of a screw press." (Boorstin, Daniel J., The Discoverers, Vintage Books, 1983.)

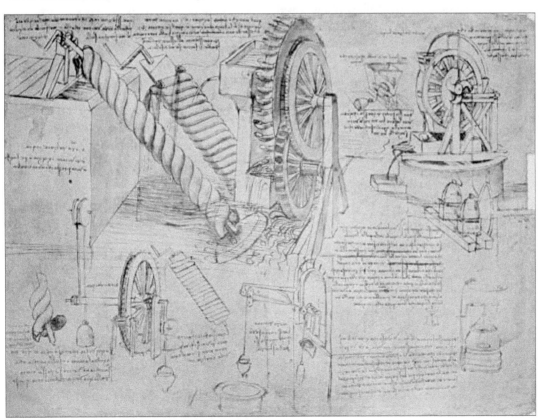

What Makes a Great Idea Log?

Sometimes, folks confuse idea logging with a scrapbook exercise. That totally misses the point. Let's talk about what design thinking is supposed to be, since a logbook is really a tool for that.

Design thinking is about visual manipulation.

A logbook should provide a space to express your ideas with as much clarity as you'd express a physical form.

Design thinking is about exploration.

A logbook should allow you to travel down multiple roads, continuously reflecting the roads you took, not merely the place you ended up.
Design thinking is about iteration.

A logbook's size is a reflection of multiple attempts, understanding that most endeavors get better with practice.

Design thinking is about capturing serendipity.

Everyone has great ideas, but great ideators actually write them down.

A logbook should effectively help you to capture your thoughts whenever and wherever you have them.

Design thinking is about making implicit thoughts explicit.

A logbook should draw out the subtler nuances inside your head onto the page so that you yourself can react to them, and surprise yourself with what you didn't know you knew.

Design thinking is about pattern identification.

A logbook should include both a plethora of material, and the application of tools to tease out the bigger picture.

Design thinking is about moving beyond initial observations to hidden insights.

A logbook should build on a thought or observation, analyzing what's presented to create greater meaning.

Interpretations

Interpretations are about making sense of what you see and turning findings into insights. Notice patterns, uncover their underlying causes, and build models to explain what's going on. Typically, these patterns are described in the form of frameworks. There are five different kinds of data that we organize into frameworks to make interpretations, in order of increasing abstraction.

- People
- Objects
- Activities
- Frames
- Needs

Intro to Interpretations

It's hard to ask people why they do the things they do. That's because most of us are unaware of the motivations that drive our actions. It's therefore critical that design researchers spend time analyzing their observations to uncover why something is happening. It's equally important to not stop at one's first explanation, but delve into even deeper causes for what's going on.

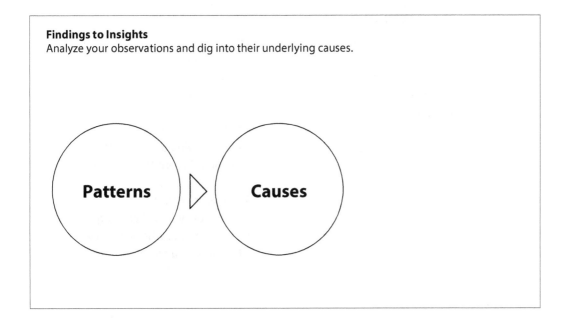

Findings to Insights
Analyze your observations and dig into their underlying causes.

Patterns ▷ Causes

Asking Five Whys

Five Whys is one of the simplest techniques for making sense of our observations.

1. Consider something you observed that you found interesting.
2. Ask why you think it happene
3. Suggest a reason.
4. Ask why you think that reason exists or why it matters.
5. Suggest an underlying reason.
6. Do this again three more times.

In each round, ensure that the reason you provide is grounded in the data. That is, check to see that the reason you give is both supported by everything else you know about the situation, and isn't disproved by another observation.

Example: A Furniture Store

"A lot of people start to hold hands when they walk into the store."

Why do they do that?
"Maybe because they want to feel closer to their partner."

Why do they want to feel closer?
"Because they're about to buy some furniture together."

Why do they need to feel closer to their partner to buy furniture?
"Because furniture is an expensive purchase you make together."

Why does that matter?
Because buying a sofa is a statement of your commitment to each other.

Why does that matter?
"Maybe how you feel walking in affects the likelihood of whether you walk out with a new sofa or not. Hmmm…"

Powers of Ten

Powers of Ten is an analysis technique for unpacking complex issues that played out at multiple scales. It's designed to make observations of both the world around you, as well your conception of the world at scales that may be unable for you to observe directly. It was developed by Rolf Faste and is based on the work of Charles and Ray Eames.

Their short film "Powers of Ten" is an animated visualization of what it would be like to view a scene from a progressively greater distance, zooming out ten times farther every ten seconds. The movie starts with a picnic in Chicago, and then zooms out to a distance where our own galaxy is visible as only a speck of light in the distance.

Returning to Earth, the camera then takes the opposite tack, zooming in closer every ten seconds, until we finally stop at the level of subatomic particles. Intended to be a dramatization of the meaning of relative scales, it's also a brilliant metaphor for observing and analyzing a situation.

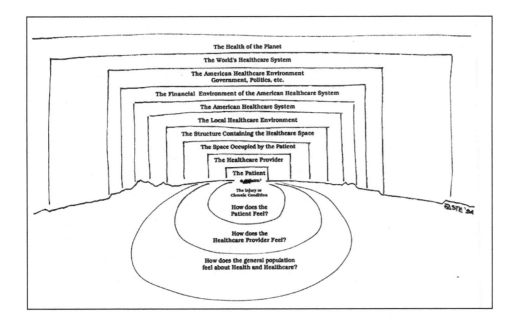

Mindmaps

You know more than you think you do. One of the challenges in Needfinding is to elicit that information so that we can understand and work with it. Mindmaps are an excellent place to start teasing out what's inside your head.

Here's a mindmap about mindmapping by Rolf Faste.

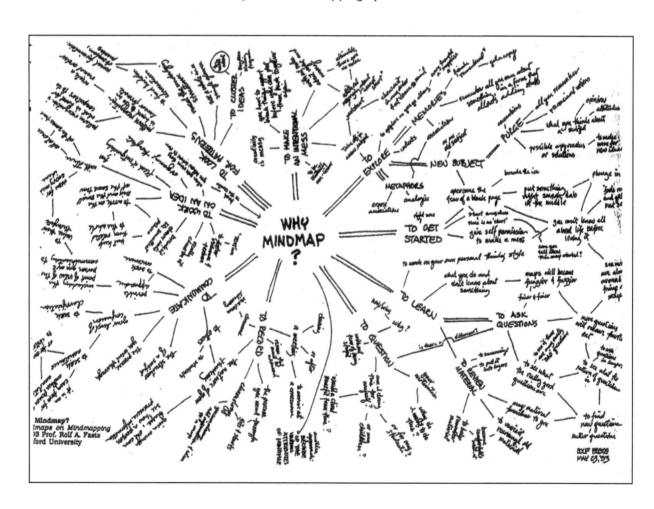

Needfinding: Design Research and Planning

Mindmapping Tips

Know your Intention

Maps can be used for a variety of purposes. These include: taking notes in real time, reconstructing an observation or conversation from memory, organizing your personal thoughts, exploring a topic or idea, and making sense out of the chaos of research findings. Note that idea-maps are DRAWINGS made with words. This is an alien concept, and will require practice to become skillful. Today's notes focus on how to explore interesting ideas.

Explore Powers of Ten

Perspective can change when you change the scale of examination. Bugs reside at the ten to the first level. Since this is where we live, it is the most comfortable level. Your maps will benefit from consciously backing out to higher levels. Think of your bug as a symptom. Back out. What is the bigger issue? Alarm clocks have to do with waking up, which has to do with sleep. Explore sleep. Dive into the problem too. We set alarms to get up at a certain times. Explore the emotional ramifications of failure. What are people's fears about being late?

Get Personal

It is a challenge to get beyond listing the cold facts that anyone might list. Feel free to write about personal experiences

and opinions. Speculate about what is going on. Write whole phrases rather than individual words. Use verbs. Describe feelings and emotions. Don't shy away from a subjective exploration of all you know. Be brave; shine a light on your subconscious thoughts.

Map the Ground

Facts comprise the physical aspects of situations. They describe the figure, form or content. Your maps become more powerful if you can also discern the context, ground, or interval. Your subject is part of a bigger system or problem. What is it? What categories are you dealing with? Are there ideas from something you read that might be useful?

Ask Questions

There is a natural tendency to only talk about what you know to be true. Your maps will benefit from exploring what you don't know. When you reach a level you are uncertain about, start asking questions. The most useful maps tend to have interesting questions all around the edges.

Invoke Stories and Metaphors

Tell stories, invoke metaphors, and make cultural references. Recall applicable fairy tales and myths. Write down personal experiences you've had that relate to your issue. Capture childhood adventures and stories about family and friends. Refer to movies you've seen, and books you've read. When you are working on a problem, your whole body is involved. Pay attention to your dreams and daydreams. Value intuitive leaps. Everything you can think of is potentially useful.

Manifest Density

Your maps will benefit from greater size and increased density. Remember the rules of brainstorming: strive for fluency and flexibility. Go for quantity: add lots of ideas, many stories, and all your thoughts. You can return to a map and Piggy-back and Leap-frog in-between what you have already done. It often happens that you run out of room just as a map begins to become interesting. Work on bigger paper. 11x17 works well because it is easy to manage after mapping and can also be photocopied.

Be Playful

Your maps will be more fun if you play with the form of the map. Make round ones. Add color. Draw lots of pictures and diagrams. Attach photos and clippings from newspapers and magazines. Work on developing a personal style. It's OK to do something different when a new subject suggests a different approach. For inspiration, look at the work of others, and at the examples provided in class. Mapping

takes time. And, there is no reason why it shouldn't be a pleasure to do. Be curious. Be playful. Have fun. Add humor. Encourage your inner child— that curious self that always asked "Why?" and was never satisfied with "Because."

Needfinding: Design Research and Planning

Mindmap Thought Starters

Still not sure how to build a Mindmap? Put down a concept that you'd like to contemplate, and start to build branches off of it. Here are some thought starters...

Powers of Ten.

Can you zoom out or in from the last word? (Ex. out might be "Pets" or in might be "Kittens"

Examples.

Are there specific illustrations of the concept? (Ex. you might "Socks" the name of your cat.)

Attributes.

Is there a particularly evocative trait? (Ex. you might "Highly Independent")

Induction.

Can you generalize the concept to what it means in the bigger picture? (Ex. "People need companions")

Deduction.

Can you infer how the concept applies to a specific case. (Ex. "Good pet for apartment dwellers.")

Cause and Effect.

Does the concept result because of something else or result in something else? (Ex. "Allergies")

Reflection.

What does the concept make you think and feel personally? (Ex. God, I hate cats)

Questions.
Does the concept provoke a particular inquiry? (Ex. "What percentage of people in the US has cats?"

Visualizing Abstract Ideas

A logbook is a great format for
representing ideas visually. Here are
some thought starters to get you going

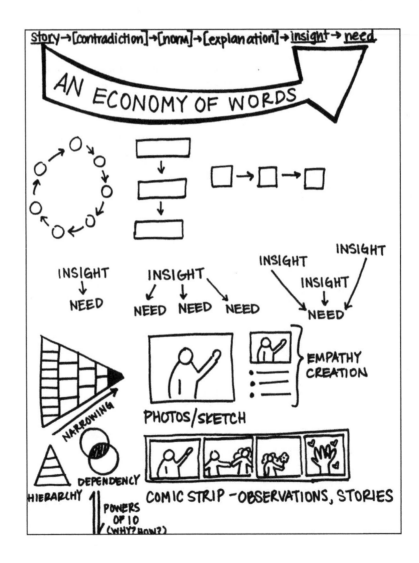

Explaining Patterns with Frameworks

A fundamental assumption of Needfinding is that the world is not a chaotic place. The phenomena that we observe adhere to repeatable patterns. Our goal is to develop new insights so we can define a course of action. While that can happen by luck and instinct, it's far more reliable to develop basic models of what we think is going on. The following pages describe some of the most common frameworks.

Creating Frameworks

- *Try multiple different kinds of frameworks: **typologies**, **timelines**, and **position maps***
- *Go **top down**: quickly make a framework and try to break it.*

- *Frameworks are about **discovery**. Ask what you learned from each framework*
- *Go **bottom up**: start with individual instances and cluster.*

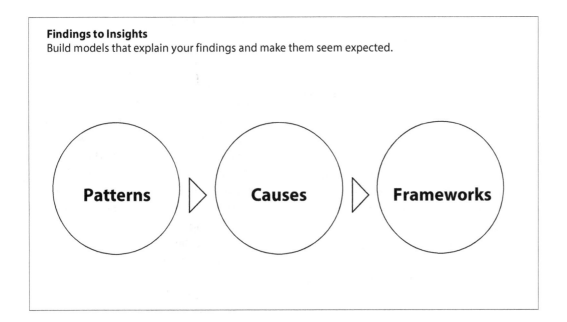

Findings to Insights
Build models that explain your findings and make them seem expected.

Patterns ▷ Causes ▷ Frameworks

Typologies

A typology is a classification of things into different categories. By "things," we can mean anything from products to behaviors to phenomena. We can then say that there are "five types of motorcycle riders" that we met, or "three different ways to use a particular product." Typologies help us to organize an otherwise bewildering amount of information into manageable clusters.

Typologies are one of the most direct ways to begin discerning patterns in our observations. Moreover, they can help take a bewildering amount of information and start to place some manageable handles around it.

Typologies are a way to develop a basic understanding that's often needed to ground and give context to further insights. There are two general approaches that you can use to create typologies…

Creating Typologies

At their core, typologies are about putting things in buckets according to their relative similarity or difference. This often happens as a simple act of sort like kinds of data into buckets according to their overall similarity. You can then name each bucket to describe what they have in common.

How many clusters should you make?

Deciding how many buckets to have depends on what's useful to you. For instance, we could classify cars by place of origin and get just two buckets, domestic and imported. That might be enough if we wanted to understand some basic dynamics of international trade. We could go further and describe them by vehicle category, such as sedan or station wagon or SUV. That might be useful if we wanted to see if there were differences in gas mileage. We could even separate those groups into sub-groups, bringing in factors such as price or size. That would certainly be helpful if we wanted to start thinking about what kind of new car to make.

Inductive Classification

For the purposes of Needfinding, it's often much more helpful for these typologies to be inductive, rather than deductive. That is to say, our goal is to let a system of classification emerge, not pick one scheme and then throw everything we have into it. That's because when we start, we often don't know whether there are three types of motorcyclists or five. That's often what we're trying to find out. Here's a basic way to get started with an inductive process to classification.

1) Assemble together some of the data that you want to work with. This can include observations from the field,

notes from a literature search, magazine clippings, or even just a brainstorm list. The more data points you have, the more exhaustive your typology will be. (And the more exhausted you might be at the end!) Then get a partner. It's a thousand times easier to do this with someone else than by yourself. "We'll do an imaginary one here."

2) Go through your data and see what's of particular interest to you. Is it a particular product? Is it a phrase from an interview? Perhaps it's a person that you observed. Let your instincts guide you to the topic that seems most interesting to you. "Okay, we've got a picture of an apple."

3) Now pick another element from your data that's of a similar type to the first. Meaning, if you picked a product, then pick another product. That's just to make sure you're not comparing "apples and oranges," which is by the way a fine comparison if you're creating a typology of fruit, which we are... "Okay, we picked an orange. We're going to leave aside the photo of Bob the fruit stand owner."

4) Now ask each other, are these two elements actually similar? Are they different? Do they represent a single "bucket?" "Yeah, they really do seem to be, well, apples and oranges. I mean, they're both round, but so are a lot of fruits. So let's make two buckets."

5) Pick up a third element and compare it to the first two. Is this a third type altogether? Or is it more like the first element and less like the second? If it is, put the first and third together. "Now we've got a lemon, which is a citrus like the orange. Sure, the orange and the apple are both round, but we've already decided that doesn't matter."

6) As you go, keep a running record of why things are similar or different. When you're done, that list might have a lot of insights on it that are actually more valuable than the typology itself. "Okay, we're not focusing on shapes. That's important."

7) Continue classifying each new element. As you do this, ask yourself if each successive element is more or less similar to the ones before it. At some point, you'll inevitably find yourselves splitting apart or merging the buckets you've already made to account for your newest addition. That's fine. In fact, that's the point. "Hmm, the citrus category seems to be less important than fruits that are sweet versus fruits that are bitter."

8) Look at the buckets you're creating and consider whether they need to be split or merged just to make them a little more balanced or useful. (If you have forty-two elements and forty-one are in one bucket and one is in another, you

may want to revisit that first bucket.) "We need to do something with this banana. Nothing seems to be like it."

9) Eventually, one of three things will happen. You might just run out of elements. Alternatively, you might just get fed up and call it good enough for government work. Hopefully, something else will happen before either of these two. If you're lucky, you'll start to find that your buckets stabilize – that they don't need to merge or split to account for each new element. You can take a breath now. "Looks like we've created eight different categories of fruits, ranging from berries to apples and pears in one category."

10) Name your buckets. Try and give a name that adequately describes what all those elements in each bucket have in common. At the same time, try to ensure that each title shows how it's different from every other title. "Berries, Sweet Citrus, hmm…what do we call this strawberry and kiwi category?"

11) Reflect on the typology you've created. What patterns have emerged?

Are there some surprises about what you've clustered together? Are certain elements that seemed totally different clustered together in the same bucket? How do you account for that? Are some buckets more filled than others? Is it a limitation of your data gathering or a reflection of a real rarity of occurrence? How would you change the typology now? "You know, I wonder how our typology would look different if we went in the middle of summer. We should go back and ask the fruit stand guys about that…"

Deductive Classification

Deductive classification starts with the big picture first, and then moves down to the individual elements. Simply put, you can try to create an overall classification system, and then use each data point to try and "break" your model. The benefit of doing this is that it's quick. The downside is that you can often create the model that your own preconceptions had assumed, and therefore fail to find anything surprising or even interesting.

Position Maps

Position maps organize disparate elements in a two by two matrix are a way to quickly understand the lay of the land. They can help show you where there are areas of intense of activity, as well as potential opportunity areas where nothing currently exists. Use matrices to organize and map the territory of potential users, observed behaviors, existing products, competing companies, new technologies, or even just relevant adjectives or descriptors.

Creating Position Maps

1) Brainstorm a list of possible attributes to use as your axes. Try as many as you can.

2) Try to keep you axes simple by avoiding multiple variables on the same scale. For example, when mapping cars, it may not be a good idea to use Sporty vs. Family-oriented as axes. After all, can't a car be sporty AND family oriented? Better to use Sporty and Not Sporty.

3) Try rating your elements on a numerical scale for each axis before putting them on the map. Their ultimate location could surprise you.

4) Think about what the extreme corners of what your map might be. Label them or make up an imaginary example or

metaphor to define those extremes if nothing currently exists there.

5) If all of your elements end up in the top right hand and bottom left hand box, it might mean that both your axes are actually measuring the same thing. Same thing for the top left and bottom right.

6) Look for gaps, patterns, clusters or ways in which elements might move over time.

7) Ask yourself what you learned.

Material Cultures

Material cultures give clues about what people do, think and feel based on their environment. The entire discipline of studying material culture concerns itself with using descriptions of objects to interpret the values, behaviors and meaning structures of the people who use them.

Physical mapping lets you figure out how someone would navigate a given location and begin to uncover what value they place on things. For example, in a store this type of exercise can help us determine what catches someone's eye; how signage, product and staff work together to create an experience.

Mapping in the home is a great way to understand how people set-up their personal living environments. To start making a Physical Map, go back to the data you collected using the AEIOU technique. This method fits perfectly into the framework level of analysis because Physical Mapping is another way to visually organize the data to tell you a story of what happens in a space and most importantly what *could* happen in a space.

Timelines

Creating a timeline is a simple way to begin to notice patterns in what you observe. Timelines can describe particular activities that people perform, objects that they interact with, or even frames of how they view the world. Timelines can describe a relatively short period of time, such as the activity of opening a package, all the way up to a long period of time, such as changes in how society views pets. Here are a few different kinds of timelines…

Out of Box Experience

One of the most rudimentary and straightforward timeline analyses a designer can do is to map out what it's like to interact with a product for the first time.

Stanford's Jim Adams is one of the people credited with developing these so-called "Out of Box Experiences." By simply photographing what it's like to go through the experience of

purchasing, opening and using a product, one can discover all sorts of successes and missed opportunities. It was this sort of study that led the first computer companies to realize that people were bewildered by the experience of opening a computer box for the first time. One easy improvement was to include a small unintimidating card that said "Read Me First." More sophisticated out of box experiences can be crafted to move beyond usability to a sense of meaning.

Consider, for example, one fan website's documentation of the ritual of opening an iPod shown below. One respondent likened it to opening a "modern day samurai sword." Such a study doesn't always have to be as thorough as this. Sometimes, a few quick sketches or cartoons in your logbook can help to reveal what's really going on.

Day in the Life

One straightforward way to understand more about a person or group of people is to outline what happens to them during the course of a typical day.

Day in the Life studies help convey a sense of routine behavior or "normal experience." They provide rich contextual information as it maps over time. At their best, Day in the Life studies can reveal patterns, tensions or contradictions that might be overlooked

Needfinding: Design Research and Planning

if one didn't compare one moment to another. A Day in the Life study can be as simple as a cartoon that you sketch in your logbook. It can also be as complex as a multi-layered document that includes both photos and detailed stories. Experts differ on whether it's better to choose an actual day to describe or create a composite out of many observations. One helpful rule of thumb: the less you know what you're looking for, the more you want to stick to the facts of what actually happened.

Era Analysis

If an Out of Box experience is one of the shortest time spans you can analyze, an Era Analysis is one of the longest. When studying larger changes in a culture, it helps to track how an entity changed and developed over time.

The types of Eras one can examine are virtually limitless. In most cases, though, the goal isn't just to describe how things were different at different times – it's to identify why things were different and why they changed. That sort of "aha" usually occurs when you start to map many different types of elements to the same era.

For instance, changes in fashion might coincide with changes in technology, and be reflected in changes in language choice for what something is called. Identifying those elements that seem to change together gets at least to correlation, if not causality.

- *Product Eras: Uncover how the role that a product played in society changed as the culture changed. For example, one could explore the change in computers from computation devices to logic devices to communication devices.*
- *Social Eras: Investigate how entities like a school or club or community changed and developed over the years. For example, the chart below shows how American's views on cats have changed over the 20th century.*
- *Technical or Commercial Eras: Show how different businesses or technologies came to have dominance in different periods. For example, one could explore the shift in retail from specialty stores to department stores to big box "category killers.*

People

People frameworks classify humans by their relative similarity. They can include user typologies, market segmentations, and demographic classifications. These people can be real or fictional, living or dead, human or otherwise. People frameworks can help you decide who to study, who to design for, or even whom to target a business towards.

Here's an example of a framework of people. It's a typology describing people at different stages of life.

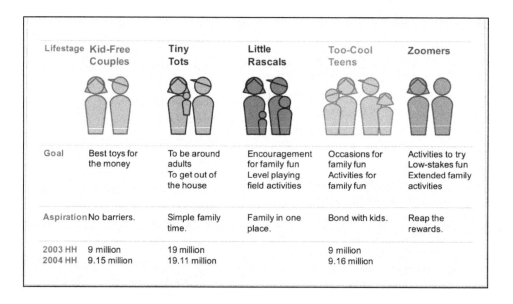

Lifestage	Kid-Free Couples	Tiny Tots	Little Rascals	Too-Cool Teens	Zoomers
Goal	Best toys for the money	To be around adults To get out of the house	Encouragement for family fun Level playing field activities	Occasions for family fun Activities for family fun	Activities to try Low-stakes fun Extended family activities
Aspiration	No barriers.	Simple family time.	Family in one place.	Bond with kids.	Reap the rewards.
2003 HH 2004 HH	9 million 9.15 million	19 million 19.11 million		9 million 9.16 million	

And this position map organizes groups of people to potentially study in order to evaluate their relevance for the project.

Objects

Object frameworks organize and classify the inanimate things you may encounter in the real world or that you might be designing. They can be as simple as the four basic food groups or as complex as a product classification system. They help reveal patterns of usage or gaps in the market.

This framework maps brands of scotch by their taste and feel. If buying a gift for a scotch lover, one could use this framework to choose something new that they would enjoy based on what they already like.

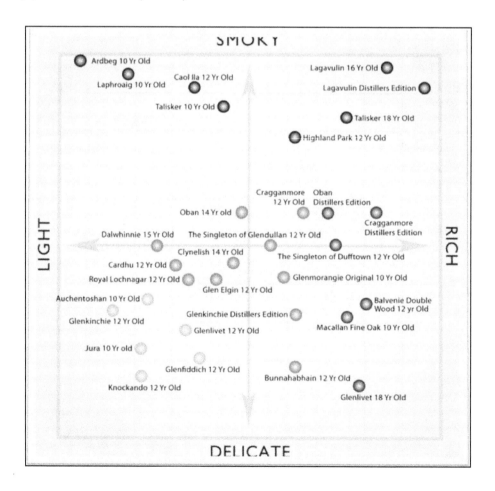

Needfinding: Design Research and Planning

This material culture maps objects in a participant's home, showing how each zone corresponds to a different function.

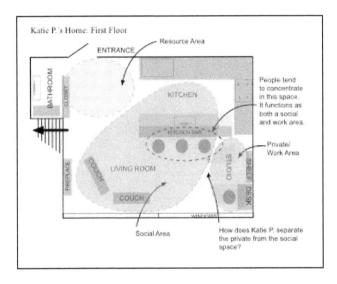

Katie P.'s Home: First Floor

ENTRANCE

Resource Area

BATHROOM

CLOSET

KITCHEN

People tend to concentrate in this space. It functions as both a social and work area.

KITCHEN BAR

Private/ Work Area

FIREPLACE

COUCH

LIVING ROOM

STUDIO

SHELF

DESK

COUCH

WINDOWS

Social Area

How does Katie P. separate the private from the social space?

Although it's not used anymore, this familiar typology once guided our food choices. It's a great example of how powerful a framework can be. Simple, clear, and accurate, it stuck in our heads and helped us create balanced meals.

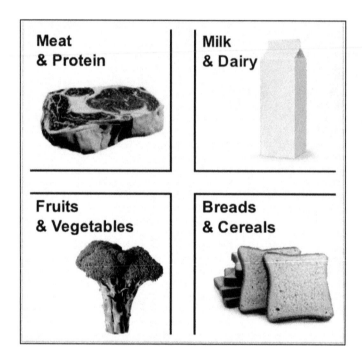

Needfinding: Design Research and Planning

Activities

Activity frameworks describe behavior or events on varying scales of time. They can range from the few seconds of opening a product for the first time, all the way to the journey of a shopping experience. Activity frameworks are useful to identify moments of delight or disappointment, the general rhythm of a user's life, or even how society has shifted from one era to the next.

This journey map shows the steps involved in purchasing a car.

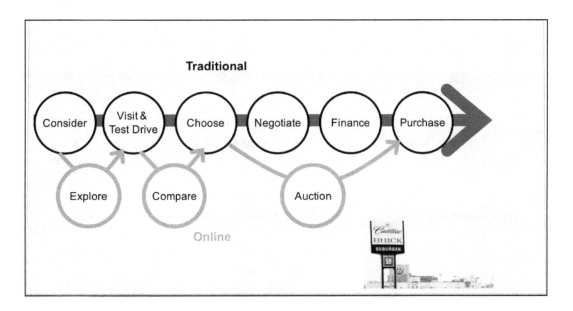

An out of box experience for an iPod breaks the interaction into individual moments.

Needfinding: Design Research and Planning

This day in the life study describes routine behavior for software developers.

[software developers]

A Day in the Life.

Software developers' interactions with physical products are limited and repetitive.
As a result, improving any single interaction has the potential to significantly
improve their work.

1. I arrive at my workstation, boot up the computer, plug in the laptop, chat with my office mate, go to the kitchen to get a snack, then come back to my desk. For the next 30 minutes, I surf the web, read the news and check e-mail.

2. I have a meeting with the development team. The chief developer brings handouts of a Gantt chart in which everyone buries their heads. After huddling around the dry erase board to solve a technical issue, we go to look at someone's computer as a group. At the end of the meeting, we put the handouts in our spiral notebooks (everyone carries one) and go back to our desks.

5. (10:40 - 11:00) I try to run an app but find that the computer needs new software. Because there isn't enough room on the hard drive, I need to install a new one. I crawl underneath the desk, unplug the tower, put it on the desk and grab the screwdriver (it's always on my desk). My office mate volunteers to help. We have questions about the device, so I go to the MIS

6. (11:00 - 11:30) I come back with the MIS guy. All three of us work on installing the new drive, putting the tower back under the desk, plugging it in and checking the diagnostics.

3. I look at my spiral notebook and decide what I need to work on today.

4. The phone rings. I first check Caller ID, then pick up the phone. I talk to another programmer and find out that there is a problem with yesterday's software build. I need to talk to the project manager, so I get up and walk over to his cubicle. We discuss how to make the necessary improvements to the code. Then I go back to my desk.

7. (11:30 - 12:00) I load the new software on the machine. Once that is complete, I boot up the new program and get acquainted with its functions.

8. (12:30 - 1:35) My friend from down the hall comes by and we go to lunch. After lunch, I take off my jacket, sit down and check e-mail. My office mate comes over. We work on a block of code together (we're trying to make a communications link work), simultaneously staring at the same screen. After a few minutes, my office mate goes back to his own desk.

Frames

To understand why people do what they do, we need to understand their **frames**: the rule sets that they use to interpret and make sense of the world.

Frames get expressed in the **narratives** that people codify and share their experiences.

Unpacking these narratives is an **interpretive act**. It requires us to examine each part of the story, identify things that are highly unusual and highly usual, and then ask why about both.

Frames: Uncovering Frames

One of the central concepts in Needfinding is that we can understand people's frames: rule sets that help people to organize the world around them. In his book *Acts of Meaning*, Jerome Bruner articulates a few key concepts that drive our understanding of frames.

Culture

Bruner says that unlike psychology, anthropology was on the right track. Culture is what really separates man and beast. Culture is really a set of agreed upon meanings. When you're born, you're showing up in the middle of a play that's been running for some time. So we very quickly figure out culture. He brings up the interesting idea that culture is a "communal tool kit" (11) that once used, makes the user a reflection of the community. (Whoa!) He quotes Clifford Geertz in saying that this is the "constituting role of culture." (12) "Human beings do not terminate at their own skins; they are expressions of a culture."

Narrative

Narratives are how we make meaning, both as individuals and societies. You take events that you experience, and organize them together into a story. You choose what to chuck and what to keep. In doing so, you make meaning. Every culture has some basic frameworks of how the world the world works, and therefore what makes people tick. "The function of the story is to find an intentional state that mitigates or at least makes comprehensible a deviation from a canonical cultural pattern. (49) These stories tell us what is normal behavior, as well as explaining abnormal behavior and phenomena when we encounter them. Importantly, it doesn't matter if the stories are factually true or not.

Framing

So how do narratives get created? This is the process of framing. When you have an experience, you alter it to fit one of your culture's "canonical representations of the social world." (56) And then you remember it. Bruner says that if it doesn't fit an existing narrative, then you either remember it because it so distinctly is an exception (for which you'll find a suitable explanation) or you'll forget about it! Framing is social. You do this so that we collectively can then know the story as well and therefore understand what's going on. These frames are our collective schema, or the organizing frames and filters through which we view the world.

The Interpretive Act

Narratives are concrete. They're descriptions of particular events, and instances of something more general. That more general rule is rarely if ever overt. Good narratives don't really hold up to logical dissection – if you want to understand why a story is the way it is, you need to interpret it. (Note: This is an idea that structural anthropologists drew from linguistics and literary theory.) Interpretive meanings are metaphorical, allusive, and context sensitive. Because order is everything in narratives, you lose the meaning when you chop up a story synchronically (i.e. putting all the car chases in one bucket.) Again, context matters. This is in contrast to "Speech Act" and "Activity Theory" social science which often chops up events into buckets.

It's Not About Truth

Bruner insists that there's no point in determining whether what we come up with is empirically provable. "Pragmatic, perspective questions would be more in order." Rather than asking if it's true, ask yourself what it would be like to believe that something were true? Marx' interpretation of all of history as a class struggle is an example he gives of something that it's irrelevant to engage on a factual level – his thinking has had a massive effect on how many people have viewed the world, and the actions that they took as a consequence. This "disregard" for the truth is not shared by all structuralists and semioticians, from whom Bruner draws a lot. Umberto Eco, for instance, believes that we have just started down the road of interpreting and testing, and he foresees a day when we'll have a small set of interpretations that will have been proved to be "true." Chew on that a bit...

Frames: Identifying Useful Narratives

Asking questions and conducting interviews will elicit stories from the people we meet. Now that we have those stories, we need to uncover their underlying meaning. To uncover needs, we extract more than what is explicitly seen or stated by listening to peoples' stories and asking why what we're hearing makes sense to the storyteller. But what parts of a long narrative should you focus on? Here are some things that might suggest a ripe area for investigation.

Contradictions

• Watching what people do, and listening to what people say about what they do, is the starting place
• The identification of inconsistencies within behavior, context, or people's stories
• The need to resolve these contradictions or inconsistencies provides opportunities for new products and services

Success and failure

• Stories describe events and contain the implicit rules that are governing people's lives
• These rules are best characterized by stories of "success" and "failure"
• To understand the "why" of a situation, one must interpret the stories of success and failure tied to that situation

Normative Statements

• Normative statements describe what's right and wrong behavior. They articulate boundaries that are revealed in: standards, morals, cover-ups, shame, shoulds, and should-nots
• Norms point to other optional behaviors, mediating strategies, or people's desire to upgrade to the norm
• People need to be perceived as normal, or have a story explaining or mediating anything outside the norm

Emotionally-Charged Moments

• Emotions often run high when people are confronted by experiences that break a particularly powerful frame or set of frames that they hold to be true.
• These moments can sometimes tip us off to rule sets that are particularly important to pay attention to.

Notable Word Choice

- We reveal how we think about something in the language that we use.
- Whether you call the inheritance tax the "estate tax" or the "death tax" says a lot about how you think about it and whether you think it's fair or not.

Your Own Reactions

- Our own reactions can often point out important differences between our own frames and those of our participants. Pay attention to your own feelings of surprise, anger, indignation or other feelings that might suggest that how you see the world is different from how other people do.

Frames: Listening for Metaphors

When people talk about their lives, we can listen for the metaphors that they use in their stories and analyze them to discern how they frame their needs, their desires, and their dreams.

As Lakoff and Johnson identified in *Metaphors We Live By*, there are basic metaphors that seem to describe how we see the world. These are conventional metaphors, called such because they describe a cultural consensus around an idea.

Becoming aware of conventional metaphors is like a fish discovering water: we're swimming in them every day, whether or not we notice them. Some linguists argue that almost all language is metaphorical. Identifying shared metaphors can help us better understand how we see the world.

Language makes extensive use of metaphors.

Argument is war: "If you use that strategy, she'll wipe you out."

Time is money: "How do you spend your time these days?"

Communication is a conduit: "I can't get that idea across to him."

Because metaphors encapsulate an idea, they can reveal and at the same time conceal. Arguments aren't literally war.

People don't usually die if they lose an argument. Time isn't money. You can't exchange "spent" time for anything. You can't really "buy" time. However, these concepts often bring along associated frames from the original idea. That's why an enterprise software system that allows employees to "trade time" with each other conceptually works.

Metaphors come in many varieties.

Structural.

Matching one concept's structure with another as with money and time. "Love is magic. Love is a physical force. Love is patient." "Relationships are a journey."

Orienting.

Associating direction with different aspects of things.
Happy is up. Sad is down. "That boosted by spirits." "You look depressed." Conscious is up. Unconscious is down. "Wake up." "He dropped off to sleep." Control is up. Lack of control is down. "Control over him." "Fall from power." Hard is up. Easy is down. "It's hard to get to the top of your profession." "He's just coasting."

Personification.

Turning other kinds of things into people.
"Cancer finally caught up with him." "Life has cheated me."

Metonymy.

Use of an attribute to substitute for a whole person or entity.
"The ham sandwich is waiting for his check."
"Acrylic has taken over the art world."

When trying to make sense of the observations and things that you hear in the field, see if it's possible to decode an underlying metaphor that recurs over and over in people's descriptions. Then, try and analyze whether your intent may be to transform that metaphor or replace it all together.

Needfinding: Design Research and Planning

Frames: Example Frameworks

Frameworks that describe mindsets or frames show differences in how people think. These can show up as different cultures, different political groups, or how people's thinking about a topic has evolved over time. A framework of mindsets or frames can highlight the differences between how designers or companies think and how ordinary people think.

This typology categorizes cars by branding and target audience. At first glance, it's a framework of objects, but it actually layers on frames as well. It's also a typology of the way people think about cars.

Utility Roadster	Upscale Carry-All	Hefty Hatchback	X-Games Offroader	Caregiver Coach	Family Adventurer
High performance	*Nice car that's bigger*	*Young and scrappy*	*Youthful and rugged*	*Amenities for your group*	*Grownup with active lives*
Cayenne; Infiniti FX	Lexus RX300, Murano, M-Class, BMW X5, Saab 9-7x	CR-V, RAV4, Element, Liberty, Saturn Vue	Xterra, Wrangler, Pick-up truck	Rendezvous, Tribeca, Pacifica	Grand Cherokee?, Touareg, 4Runner, LR Discovery

Rugged Hauler	Safe Schoolbus	Stylish Shuttle	Palace on Wheels	Safari Offroader
Be outdoors, solo or group	*No frills safety and utility*	*More stylish minivan*	*Pamper the posse*	*Ultra capable yet refined.*
Explorer, Durango?, Sequoia, Pathfinder, Crew-cab truck	Highlander, Pilot, minivans	MDX, XC90, MX5	Escalade, Aviator, H2, Aspen	LR3, H1, H3, Commander

This era analysis shows how the way we see cats has changed over time.

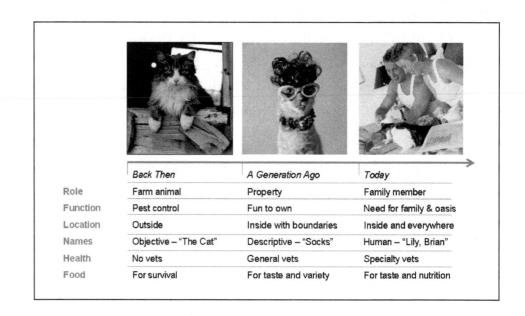

	Back Then	A Generation Ago	Today
Role	Farm animal	Property	Family member
Function	Pest control	Fun to own	Need for family & oasis
Location	Outside	Inside with boundaries	Inside and everywhere
Names	Objective – "The Cat"	Descriptive – "Socks"	Human – "Lily, Brian"
Health	No vets	General vets	Specialty vets
Food	For survival	For taste and variety	For taste and nutrition

Needfinding: Design Research and Planning

Needs

Look for **needs** (verbs) not **solutions** (nouns).

Needs don't exist in isolation. Every need is related to a **network** of needs, more or less specific than itself.

Needs can be **explicit** or **implicit**. Revealing implicit needs requires an act of grounded interpretation.

Not all needs are created equal. Needs can be **widely** or **narrowly** shared. Common needs can seem profound, while lower needs can be useful for designing products.

Ask **why** to discover more general needs. Ask **how** to discover more specific ones.

Needs: Implicit vs. Explicit

It's said that "people can't tell you what they really need." This statement may be true, but if you listen carefully to their stories, people will give you unmistakable clues which reveal their needs. Some needs are explicit, while others are implicit. Explicit needs reside in the realm of our awareness. Implicit needs lie deeper, and often we are not even aware of their presence.

Explicit needs

- *Needs that we can observe or discuss.*
- *Are directly perceived by the observer or expressed by the one with the need. Can be understood directly by listening to what people say and observing what people do.*

Implicit needs

- *Needs we might be unaware of.*
- *Are not directly perceived by the one with the need, and require an active and creative interpretation.*
- *Are buried and can be understood indirectly through the stories that people tell.*

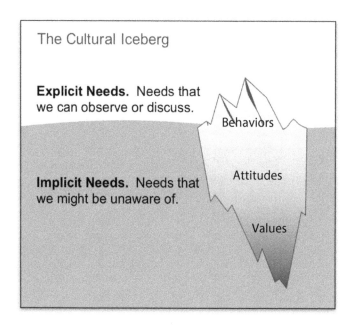

The Cultural Iceberg

Explicit Needs. Needs that we can observe or discuss.

Behaviors

Implicit Needs. Needs that we might be unaware of.

Attitudes

Values

Needs vs. Solutions

A need is a physical, psychological or cultural requirement that people have. In its most basic form, a need is something that's missing. Describing a situation as a need can open up all sorts of possibilities for innovation.

Supply and Demand

In many ways, the distinction between needs and solutions is as fundamental to the practice of innovation as the concept of supply and demand is to economics. Just imagine that you were working on a project for a ladder manufacturer. You could spend all day brainstorming new ladders, and many of your ideas might be better than what's currently on the market. However, if you focused on the needs that ladders solved, you might instead brainstorm ideas to, for instance, help someone reach a high shelf. You might then come up with all sorts of novel solutions that rendered ladders themselves obsolete.

Needs are verbs.
Solutions are nouns.

Separating out needs and solutions is critical. The easiest way to make sure

you do is to try this simple rule of thumb: state needs as verbs, and solutions as nouns. People need *to reach a high shelf*. They then choose the solution of *a ladder*.

Similarly, beware of using nouns like "the need for convenience" or "She needs comfort." These sorts of phrases often guarantee that you're describing needs in a way that's so general or abstract as to be useless for design.

Not all needs are directly observable.

Explicit needs are directly perceived by the needfinder or expressed by the needer. Implicit needs are not directly perceived by the needer and require an active creative interpretation by the needfinder. Like an iceberg, there's a lot that's beneath the surface.

Needs: Maslow's Hierarchy

Abraham Maslow, developed the first coherent classification of needs that was relevant to conditions in modern society. At the same time, that hierarchy of needs offered a uniform level of generality. Maslow's Hierarchy isn't specific enough to directly help product developers. That said, it provides the impetus for considering the larger context of observations.

Self Actualization Needs. Seeking fulfillment for self and giving to others, etc.

Esteem Needs. Ego, self-respect, autonomy, status, recognition and attention, etc.

Social Needs. Affection, belonging, acceptance, friendship, etc.

Safety Needs. Security, protection from physical and emotional harm, etc.

Physiological Needs. Hunger, thirst, shelter, sex, etc.

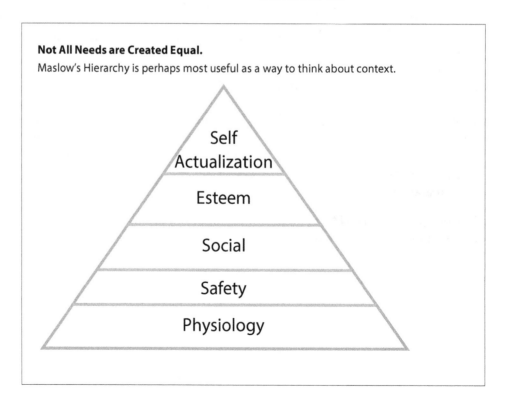

Not All Needs are Created Equal.
Maslow's Hierarchy is perhaps most useful as a way to think about context.

Needs: Hierarchy for Design

Some needs are purely a result of the current scenario, and will disappear when the prevailing situation changes. Others are created by the solutions to other needs. The most universal needs suggest deep seated, longer lasting problems that may not be fixed by a single solution. In this way, needs can be characterized by their connection to current solutions, situations or behaviors.

Common Needs

Common Needs exist for most people in most situations over the long term. They are the most fundamental and universal needs that people face, being almost a basic fact of life. Most of us need to socialize, even though we may satisfy this need in different ways, producing different Activity Needs. Our Common Needs are much the same. Individuals are usually aware of Common Needs, but they routinely try to have these needs met by meeting the more immediate Activity or Context Need. When people articulate these needs, they often describe them as one of the things you just have to live with. Otherwise, they may not perceive Common Needs at all, and may regard worrying about such things as a waste of time.

Context Needs

Context Needs are a result of the situation in which people live, work or operate. The same need will exist for people operating in the same industry, profession, region, culture, etc. While Activity Needs are characterized as specific actions, such as drinking coffee, Context Needs are more goal-oriented, such as the need to have a pleasant experience. People may not perceive or immediately articulate their Context Needs, in part because they are so pervasive.

Activity Needs

Activity Needs are the result of specific activities that a person performs or wants to perform. They are the same for all people who want to the same thing. Like Qualifier Needs, Activity Needs may disappear if current solutions are made obsolete. People are often aware of their Activity Needs, although they may describe them in terms of existing product or service solutions.

Qualifier Needs

Qualifier Needs represent the most immediate types of needs that people face. They are often a result of problems with existing solutions. The same Qualifier Needs exist for all people who use a particular set of solutions in similar ways. People are likely to be aware of Qualifier Needs, and, if asked, may describe such needs in terms of changes or additions to specific qualities of a product or service.

Not All Needs are Created Equal.
Often, context and activity needs are the most useful for design.

Common	**Need to be loved.**	Needs of nearly everyone.
Context	**Need to get married.**	Needs of people of the same age, profession, region, etc.
Activity	**Need to go on a date.**	Needs of people in the same context who want to do the same thing.
Qualifier	**Need to hold a hot cup without spilling.**	Needs of people in the same context who want to do the same thing, the same way.

Needfinding: Design Research and Planning

An Example of a Needs Hierarchy

As part of a project for the watchmaker Casio, a team was studying how people manage different frames on time. It turns out that Einstein was right – time is relative! These different perspectives can lead to conflict between people as they try to navigate each others different perspectives.

As part of their research, the team interviewed a young man named Michael. He told them about his ex-girlfriend, Beth, and about how they were always getting into arguments. Many of these arguments stemmed from different views of time.

"I would tell Beth that I would meet her at 7:30," he related. "And she would always say, 'Do you mean *your* 7:30 or *my* 7:30? Because your 7:30 could be 8:00.'" This conflict revealed all sorts of needs that Michael had.

The following diagram shows some of the needs that the team explored in creating a Needs Hierarchy for Michael. Based on the hierarchy, the team decided that the most interesting solutions involved changing the experience of meeting up. The result was an easy way for friends and couples to update each other as they were en route.

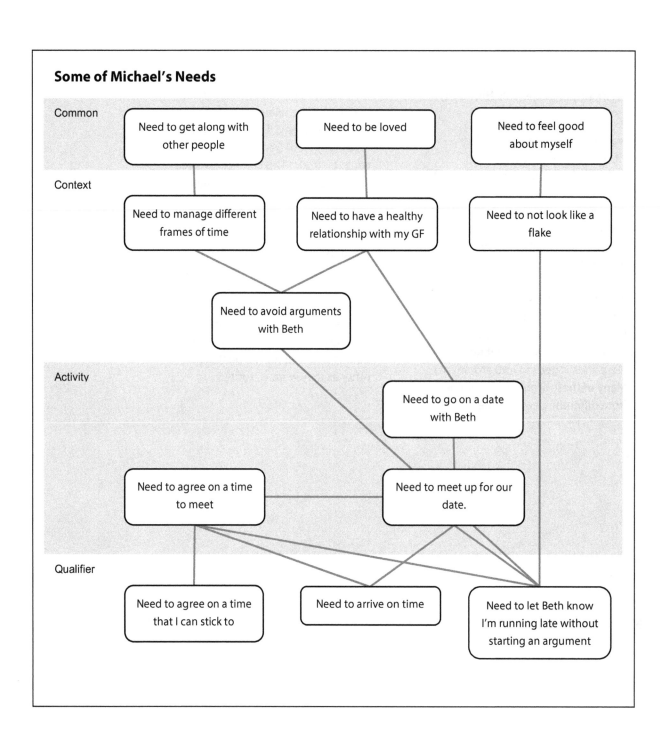

Some of Michael's Needs

Common

Need to get along with other people

Need to be loved

Need to feel good about myself

Context

Need to manage different frames of time

Need to have a healthy relationship with my GF

Need to not look like a flake

Need to avoid arguments with Beth

Activity

Need to go on a date with Beth

Need to agree on a time to meet

Need to meet up for our date.

Qualifier

Need to agree on a time that I can stick to

Need to arrive on time

Need to let Beth know I'm running late without starting an argument

Directions

Creating directions is about turning insights into actions and determining appropriate approaches for design. Define what good looks like at varying levels of detail. There are five different kinds of directive information that we can create, in order of increasing concreteness and specificity.

- Imperatives
- Design Principles
- Pattern Languages
- Metaphors
- Criteria

Needfinding: Design Research and Planning

Intro to Directions

A rich body of insights will be able to describe where a company can go. However, it is critical to not just describe but to prescribe where to go next. A complex strategy can boil down to a few concrete directions.

Different Levels of Directions.

Billy set up his lemonade stand on a path frequented by bicyclists, runners, and skaters. He realized that he could best serve his customers if he worried about what they worried about. That means helping them finish their journey.

Imperatives	Design Principles	Products & Services
Refresh. Help people replenish their energy.	Make drinks that supply energy. Offer people ways to cool down. Provide drinks to people who don't stop.	Lemonade Electrolyte powder in drinks Power bars Mist generator Oxygen tank
Inspire. Inspire people to go the distance.	Make trips feel like an event. Inspire people before they start, along the trail, and at the stand.	Morning wakeup calls Inspirational messages on the path Supportive staff
Contact. Give people a place to check in.	Help people get in touch. Give people info to plan trips. Provide alternate checkpoints.	Phone message services Weather forecast posted News updates through radio Door-to-door collection
Aid. Accidents occur. Help people get moving again.	Help people who may be hurt. Help fix equipment that may be broken.	First aid kit Bike repair kit Bike pump Inline skate parts Maps of the park
Direction Help people decide where to go.	Help people change their trip. Help people plan their next trip. Help people who are lost.	Trail advice Workout guides Directions

---

Imperatives

Imperatives are short, memorable statements that express what a designer has to do. They encapsulate the learnings and give strategic direction. A successful solution will address multiple, if not all, imperatives at once.

What A Great Imperative Does

Clearly articulates a coherent vision.

Great imperatives provide a clear picture of what the future can be. To be clear and visionary, imperatives need to be crisp, concise, and use powerful words. The phrase needs to capture an entire thought, not just part of one.

Uses metaphors.

It can be very challenging to provide a new vision in a concise way. Metaphors are a great way to show how the world can look and feel by capturing a lot of content in an easily understandable and shareable package.

Is unique to the company.

Great imperatives contain information that is specific to the company and its particular situation. They leverage a company's unique strengths and help create differentiated experiences. They are not generic statements that can be applied to just any other business.

Includes short and long-term implications.

Imperatives don't provide specific solutions to problems — they provide underlying principles for how to solve them. Consequently, they can address short-term problems while guiding initiatives that are farther out.

Tells you what to do.

A great imperative is a statement of action — it tells you what to do in unambiguous terms. It is not a descriptive commentary. While imperatives reside at a high level, they are nonetheless focused on things that are specific and actionable. They provide a base for an entire vision of products, services, sales, research and messaging.

Tips for Writing Imperatives

Make it actionable, and actively voiced.

Phrase the imperative in the positive, first, saying what to do using concrete language. If needed, use a negative instruction after the positive. Example: "Think Picnic, not Marathon." .

Keep it short, sweet, and sticky.

An idea that is succinctly and compellingly stated can be more easily memorized and spread throughout an organization.

Ground imperatives with insight.

An imperative without insights to back it up is an assertion. Powerful imperatives are defensible when then they build on insights about people's needs and the capabilities of the client.

Use multiple methods.

Following a research-based, sequential, observations-to-frameworks-to-imperatives process works, but so does mining our ideas at each stage for the implicit genius of gut feel.

Excite the imagination.

Compelling imagery and metaphor can often communicate complex ideas and powerful emotion far better than literal commands, especially when synthesizing several design principles elegantly.

Design Principles

Design principles are general strategies for solving a design problem, independent of the particular solution. Design principles have long existed among architects, designers and engineers. They serve as heuristics about what seems to work.

The Golden Mean

The Golden Mean, or Golden Ratio, is a great example of a design principle that has been used for millennia. It describes two segments, where the ratio of the short segment to the long segment is equal to the ratio of the long segment to the sum of both segments. Nautilus shells display this proportionality, as does the Parthenon, the Great Pyramid at Giza and Stonehenge. Renaissance designers such as DaVinci were captivated the Golden Mean's beauty, and incorporated it into their works. The original iPod used the same proportions. At 2.125" by 3.375", even credit cards approximately follow the Golden Mean.

The Principle of Mapping
Mapping is a fairly universal design principle. It says that things are easier to use when there's a clear relationship between a set of controls and their resulting effects. In the case of these stovetops, that's achieved by mimicking the size and arrangement of the controls and burners.

Bad   Better   Best

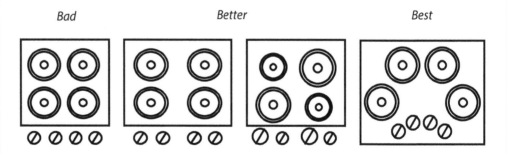

What Makes a Great Principle?

A great design principle tells you how to do something without constraining to a single solution. For instance, Mapping helps you make stoves easier to use, but it doesn't design the stove for you.

Creating Design Principles

An easy way to create design principles is to ideate new solutions and abstract out why they're great. Even if a solution is lousy, saying why articulates the principle it violates.

Universal vs. Specific Principles

As a problem gets more complicated, we need more specific guidelines tailored to particular contexts. For instance, if you want to design a family of power tools, it's useful to describe materials and forms that convey a ruggedness, durability or power.

Of course, as you start to describe particular aspects of design, no single principle covers everything. What emerges is a system of design principles that all work together coherently to reflect an understanding of a system's major needs and the most effective way to solve them.

Some Great Universal Principles

The Golden Ratio

Objects feel "balanced" when the ratio of their width to their height is equal to the ratio of their height to the sum of both segments.

Mapping

Use visual similarities between controls and their outcomes to clarify cause and effect.

Graded Controls

The level of control offered by a system should be proportional to the level of proficiency of the people using the system.

Some Great Specific Principles

Clean Flooring Materials

In food retail, use surface materials that seem clean even when they're dirty, such as slate. Avoid materials that seem dirty even when clean, like linoleum.

The Pancake Principle

Leave out key ingredients from prepared foods to give folks the sense that they're really cooking.

Pattern Languages

Design principles can be combined together to achieve a larger effect. In this way, they can act like individual nouns and verbs in a sentence. For this reason, designers have come to regard such systems as Pattern Languages.

The idea of a pattern language was first developed in the mid-seventies by Christopher Alexander. A professor of Architecture at UC Berkeley, Alexander set out to find a way of codifying implicit knowledge about how people solve recurring problems when they go about building things. He and his colleagues tried to capture a set of basic design principles, or patterns. For example, architects know that one way to make a room that's great for children is to include a sixteen inch high step that runs along the perimeter of the room. Kids use the step to sit on, as a table, and even a stage. Alexander's team wrote up this information about what made a great room for children, in the form of simple set of guidelines with examples.

The resulting book, entitled "A Pattern Language," included 253 different patterns about solutions that were known to work. Part of each pattern is a description of how those principles are supposed to connect with the other principles in the book. The patterns begin at the largest scale, describing the ideal placement of a town.

Each successive pattern describes a more detailed topic, and the book works its way down to neighborhoods, streets, buildings, and eventually rooms. Pattern 251, for example, is entitled "Different Chairs." It describes why it's better to use a variety of chairs in a room, some big, some small, with some softer than others as shown below.

In many ways, the real value in "A Pattern Language" is the intellectual exercise; the level of detail and thoroughness that Alexander's team achieved is far beyond what most of us need to get the job done. It nonetheless pointed the way for people to think of design principles in a systematic way. In particular, computer programmers and interface designers realized that idea of pattern languages provided them with a way to create extensible building blocks for solving a variety of different applications. Patterns in programming suggested how to write reusable code that programmers could call upon when needed. The last few years have witnessed the emergence of several languages for improving web design.

For the rest of us, pattern languages provide a framework for develop design principles. We probably don't need something as sophisticated as Alexander's pattern language. We could, however, seek to create a system to help us develop insights around a particular category of users, and then tailor the resulting actions to the needs of different particular design instances.

Pattern Languages

Christopher Alexander first developed pattern languages as a way of describing and making explicit common solution strategies that designers and architects have developed over time.

Principle 251: Different Chairs

When you are ready to furnish rooms, choose the variety of furniture as carefully as you have made the building so that each piece of furniture, loose or built in, has the same unique and organic individuality as the rooms and alcoves have, each different according to the place occupied…never furniture any place with chairs that are identically the same…

Metaphors

Prescriptive metaphors serve to encapsulate an otherwise complex notion of how we aim to change a situation. They express multiple relationships through a single, initially disconnected comparison.

Designers have used such metaphors for years, often in implicit ways that just felt right. It's nonetheless possible to identify specific metaphors that we may deliberately choose because of their appropriateness for a specific design problem. When considering new solutions, you might choose to first articulate the overarching metaphor that you're seeking to give form to.

What Makes a Great Metaphor?

Great design metaphors are ones that help create better designs. As such, try and make your metaphors:

Self-explanatory.

You get it the minute you hear it without explanation. Don't use metaphors that have multiple or contradictory meanings.

Evocative.

Ideas start popping into your head about what the solution could be. Discard a metaphor if nothing comes to mind when you hear it.

Useful.

It provides clear direction for what's in and what's out. Test your metaphor by getting people to say what design principles they suggest.

Disconnected.

It draws from a world that's different from your own. Don't use cars as metaphors for designing cars. Use animals, clothing or sports!

Appropriate.

It's tailored to the audience who'll use it. For instance, engineers tend to like product metaphors. Marketers tend to like activity metaphors.

Using Metaphors to Inspire Design

While descriptive or conventional metaphors describe underlying ways in which people see the world, prescriptive metaphors articulate complex ideas about how we may wish to change it.

An otherwise unrelated idea about sunflowers...

...captured the desired look and feel of the flat-panel iMac.

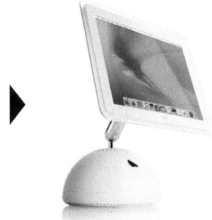

Criteria

Design criteria are the most concrete type of directions. They are requirements that a solution must meet that leave no room for interpretation like design principles do. Benchmarks, standards, regulations, and constraints are all different kinds of design criteria.

When we set out to built the Sonim phone, there were no standards for a phone this rugged. So we had to create them. Compiled from over ten years of feedback from customers that lead extreme and rugged lifestyles, the Rugged Performance Standards consist of 12 benchmarks of endurance that set the standard to which all rugged devices must live up to.

SONIM'S RUGGED PERFORMANCE STANDARDS

EXTRA-LONG BATTERY LIFE

ACCESSIBLE KEYPAD

EXTRA-LOUD SPEAKER

PROTECTION FROM MICROPARTICLES

WATERPROOF

PROTECTION FROM DROPS

RESISTANT TO SHOCKS & VIBRATIONS

RESISTANT TO EXTREME TEMPERATURES

RESISTANT TO EXTREME PRESSURE

RESISTANT TO PUNCTURES

RESISTANT TO OILS AND CHEMICALS

3-YEAR COMPREHENSIVE WARRANTY

Solutions

The solutions phase of the process is about creating the tangible product, service or system to fill the need. It's about making concepts tangible so you can have an impact and get feedback. Doing this is really a whole book in itself, and we therefore can't cover all of it here. There are six different kinds of solutions that designers create.

- Products
- Services
- Messages
- Environments
- Experiences
- Businesses

Intro to Solutions

Developing meaningful opportunities calls for finding elegant solutions that have meaning for people because they connect with their everyday life. A successful solution will be grounded in needs and address multiple imperatives. Creating a solution involves generating ideas, refining them into high-fidelity concepts, and developing plans to make them real.

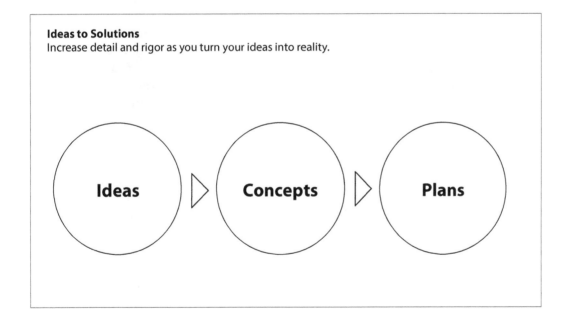

Ideas to Solutions
Increase detail and rigor as you turn your ideas into reality.

Ideation

The real value of ideating goes well beyond just coming up with potential solutions. Often, the act of creating a solution taps into our tacit knowledge, showing things that we may not have explicitly thought or discussed. By analyzing the ideas we've generated, we can learn even more about the insights, frameworks, imperatives and solutions we have created.

Ideation Habits

To create great solutions, be prolific in your ideation. Consistently coming up with great ideas isn't luck. With the right practices, environments, and habits, we can all get better at generating ideas. In 1998, Jump Associates conducted a study to identify the common habits used by people known for their breakthrough ideas. That research produced the following Ten Habits of Great Ideators.

1. Start with a need.

It was Ben Franklin who said "Necessity is the mother of invention," a principle he applied throughout his life to a host of innovations that are impressive for their breadth and variety, as well as their ingenuity.

2. Create a supportive environment.

The iconoclastic designer Yoshiro Nakamats has created an extremely personalized, sophisticated environment to stimulate and nurture his creativity, including sensory deprivation tanks and special stereo goggles that project patterns intended to put him into his creative sweet spot.

3. Gather different voices.

Virginia Woolf presided over an anti-university of artists, critics, and writers. Called the Bloomsbury Group, they were notorious rebels against Victorian Era inhibitions in art, literature, and sex.

4. Ask stupid questions.

Great Ideators often prompt their own thinking by asking questions that others might find to be a waste of time. Albert Einstein had a knack for asking very good questions that were deceptively simple and childlike. His question, "What would it be like to ride a beam of light?" led to his Theory of Relativity.

5. Feed your head.

Charles Darwin was astute not only in his observations, but also in his own process of learning and relating to the world around him. For him, travel involved seeing diverse data and making connections.

6. Encourage wild ideas.

Walt Disney pushed his creative staff to over-the-top designs for Disneyworld installations and movie plots. He continually challenged his team to come up with new ideas, to amuse and amaze him; according to several accounts he demanded independent and daring thinking outright.

7. Go for quantity.

The best way to have great ideas is to have a lot. Quantity yields quality. Pablo Picasso said, "The fact that I paint such a large number of studies is simply part of my manner of working. I do a hundred studies in a few days, whereas another painter might spend a hundred days on a single painting. By carrying on, I will open windows. I will go behind the canvas, and perhaps something will be brought out."

8. Keep an idea log.

Everyone has great ideas. Great Ideators write them down. Leonardo da Vinci's notebooks are the manifestations of an extraordinarily creative, inquisitive mind. We've already discussed idea logs at length. As an ideation tool, they're invaluable.

9. Use the buddy system.

Paul McCartney has often used the song "Getting Better" as an example of the friction that fueled his partnership with John Lennon: "All I remember is that I said, 'It's getting better all the time,' and John contributed the legendary line, 'It couldn't get much worse,' which I thought was very good. Against the spirit of that song, which was all super-optimistic — then there's that lovely little sardonic line: Typical John."

10. Make bad ideas better.

Thomas Edison's motto was, "There is a better way. Find it!" In his description inventing the kinetiscope, he said, "All I have done is to perfect what has been attempted before, but did not succeed.

Ideation Media

Marshall McLuhan famously said that the medium is the message. And it's true. How you express an idea will drastically affect how you and others think about it. Some media will drive you to comprehensive detail, while others will encourage you to go shallow but wide in your ideation.

Idea Logs

Idea logs are a great way to let your mind explore various solutions. They're particularly effective when you're not yet quite sure what the problem is that you're trying to solve.

Lists

A rapid-fire generation of ideas in list form is particularly useful in groups when you want to produce a large number of ideas that can be further developed later on.

Post-It Notes

It can be helpful to use Post-It notes when you're looking to generate a lot of ideas that can't be captured in words on a list. Post-Its also have the advantage of being sortable after you're done.

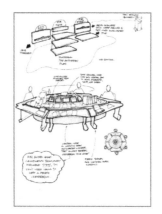 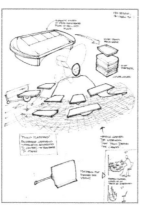 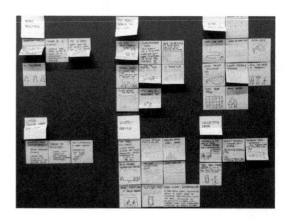

Half Sheets

One of the most important issues in ideation is how much detail to provide. Too little, and an idea's real merit may be obscured. Too much, and a team can get dragged into implementation questions that are being asked too early.

In 1999, Jump Associates pioneered a simple yet surprisingly useful medium for ideation: 8½"X5½" sheets of paper and sharpie markers.

The approach forced the team to flesh out an idea with just enough information to provide necessary detail, but confining enough to ensure that one didn't get bogged down on a single idea.

Half sheets have rapidly become the de facto standard for new product ideation when designers are seeking to explore an area broadly.

When you want to go a little deeper into your ideas than what Post-It notes can offer, but aren't ready to explore every detail, try using half sheets. Give every half sheet a title, a simple sketch, and maybe a caption to call out an important detail or two. That's it.
Don't spend more than a minute or so on each individual idea.

For a hardware product…

For a food product…

For an online product…

Marker Pad Sheets

When you have a clear idea of the solution space, and you'd like to explore the physical form of a particular concept in greater detail, try using a large marker pad. This will allow you to tear out sheets and post them up to compare and combine elements together.

Needfinding: Design Research and Planning

Storyboards

New service and business innovations often require designers to show how a situation will change over time. Even for a single product, it may be helpful to describe a particular scenario of use. In those situations, storyboards can be incredibly helpful.

A storyboard can vary in sophistication, from a simple comic strip, to the kind of detailed sketches used by professional animators to frame out a movie.

UNIFY: USE
Four steps drive instant team payment on the fly.

FORM YOUR TEAM.

Bob opens a "Ski Trip" team instantly from his iPhone and invites friends from his social network. Bob and friends plan out the trip's big expenses and determine their contribution caps. They agree on a plan.

- Team member profiles with option to link to social networks
- Real-time, instant credit checks
- Team member selection via proximity sensors, and push notification

SET YOUR RULES.

Before they start making any purchases, the team agrees who has spending power. Since they're good friends, anyone can buy, but for less tight-knit groups where security is a priority, a team might set rules so only the organizers can make big purchases.

- Planning coordination synchs to iCal, Outlook, and Google Calendar
- Graphic budgeting
- Flexible purchasing rules

GET THINGS DONE.

Bob uses Unify to book a cabin, and it automatically distributes the cost across the group. Meanwhile, Jack buys a week's worth of groceries for the whole team. This too is split across the group. He also picks up a nice bottle of scotch, but only divides that cost across a select few members.

- One-touch 2D barcode purchase
- Sub-team payment selection
- Overpay push alerts

EVEN UP.

When the trip is finished, the team is able to track their spending, settle up any discrepancies, and then close out the account instantly. Unify will maintain the group's history, for easy access in case they want to take a similar trip in the future.

- Even-up across team with wired reimbursements
- Performance and habit tracking
- Instant account close
- Individual histories

29

Products: Concepts

A product concept is a more developed form of an idea. It describes some of the key questions that consumers might have, and is therefore helpful for initial product testing. Product concepts typically have a few common elements.

1. Concept Name

Give your concept an evocative name that captures the feeling of the idea. *E.g. "iPod."*

2. Tagline

A great tagline answers the two most basic questions someone might have about a new concept: What is It? Why is it good? *E.g. "A digital music player that lets you fit a thousand songs in your pocket."*

3. Image

A picture says a thousand words. Provide an image of what your concept will ideally look like. *E.g. The iPod photo*

4. Core Need

Give a description of who the concept is primarily intended for and the most important need that you think it will solve. *E.g. "For young people, music isn't just something they listen to. It's the soundtrack of their life. They need to be able to take that soundtrack wherever they go."*

5. Point of Difference

Tell your audience why this concept is different and better than other things that might be available today. *E.g. "Other MP3 players work like computers. This works like a cassette player, so it's simple to use…" etc.*

Needfinding: Design Research and Planning

6. Reason to Believe

Every claim of a concept brings up new questions, as to whether something will actually solve the stated need or be truly different. Explain why your concept is more than just a pipedream. *E.g. "The iPod's hard drive is 5GB, big enough to store 1000 songs in the industry standard in 160-Kbps MP3 format. And the battery provides 10 hours of life, so you can literally take it anywhere."*

7. Partnerships

Don't always go it alone. The more complicated the business model, the harder it may be to pull off solo. Generate a list of partners that may have complementary offerings, and build cooperative relationships with them.

8. Critical Assets

Consider all of the critical resources needed to make the concept a reality, and how to get those resources, whether it is through partnerships, acquisitions, or grounds-up capability building.

7. Implementation Details

Depending on the type of product, you may want to include critical supporting information about pricing and variations, sizes, flavors, etc. *E.g. "Price: $399."*

Here's a mockup of what a concept writeup for the original iPod might have looked like. It obviously doesn't include every technical specification, just the details that designers, marketers and consumers would most want to know so that they could understand and evaluate the concept.

iPod

A digital music player that lets you fit a thousand songs in your pocket.

For young people, music isn't just something they listen to. It's the soundtrack of their life. They need to be able to take that soundtrack wherever they go.

Other MP3 players work like computers. This works like a cassette player, so it's simple to use. A unique "Scroll Wheel" controller allows for easy one handed operation. And because iPod is made by Apple, it connects directly with iTunes on your Mac, so you can sync all the CDs you've already burned.

The iPod's hard drive is 5GB, big enough to store 1000 songs in the industry standard in 160-Kbps MP3 format. And the battery provides 10 hours of life, so you can literally take it anywhere.

Price: 5GB $399/ 10GB $499

Products: Systems

A system logic is a company's philosophy of customer needs and how it can organize its offerings to meet those needs. It's an underlying framework that guides and choreographs every element of what a company offers, characterizing both the practices of the business and the behavior of its customers. While a system logic can often be expressed in a simple phrase, such as "coffee culture," such a description usually requires some first-hand experience in order to be fully understood. From such an understanding, more-specific themes can evolve that guide the creation of new products and services, and in turn reinforce the logic.

Type of Solution	Starbucks	Lego	Nike	Apple
System Logic				
A method to organize offerings based on needs	Coffee culture	A modular kit of parts	High-performance individualist athleticism	The Macintosh look and feel
Families				
Offerings that work together to meet a variety of needs	Retail shops In-store products Grocery store products	Legoland Duplo	Nike Goddess ACG gear (footwear, clothes, eyewear) Dri-fit sportswear	iMac iBook Power Mac Powerbook
Offerings				
Solutions that completely replace current products and services	Frappuccino Tiazza Jazz CDs Books	Lego Mindstorms Spaceship sets Castle sets Pirate coves sets	Air Jordan Shoes Air Warp skates Tiger Woods golf balls Dri-fit Tech top	Power Mac G4 iPod Airport wireless cards
Features				
New products and services that incorporate some form of incremental improvement	Dark roasted coffee Cappuccinos to go Coffee ice cream	Wheels, flags, swords, and other ways to "theme" building blocks	Air insole Nylon upper Tread pattern Contoured footbed	G4 microprocessor Titanium casing Appealing aesthetics Firewire connections

Needfinding: Design Research and Planning

Businesses: Revenue Models

There aren't thousands of ways to make money. There are actually only eight. Use these revenue models to come up with new ways to turn your idea into a business concept.

Unit Sales

Sell a product or service to customers. Examples: GE, Nike, P&G, Intel, Dell.

Advertising Fees

Sell opportunities to distribute messages.
Examples: Google, *The New York Times*, network television, baseball parks.

Franchise Fees

Sell and support a replicable business for others to invest in, grow, and manage locally. Examples: McDonald's, Edison Electric, Amazon store front.

Utility Fees

Sell goods and services on a per-use or as-consumed basis.
Examples: PG&E,water, cellular, ASPs.

Subscription Fees

Charge a fixed price for access to your services for a period of time or series of uses. Examples: 24-Hour Fitness, ISPs, Rhapsody Music, consumer reports.

Transaction Fees

Charge a fee for referring, enabling, or executing a transaction between parties. Examples: Visa, Charles Schwab, eBay, Google ads, real-estate brokers.

Professional Fees

Provide professional services on a time-and-materials contract. Examples: H&R Block, healthcare professionals, architects, designers.

License Fees

Sell the rights to use intellectual property. Examples: San Francisco Giants,
university technology, biotech labs.

Acknowledgements

This book draws on the ideas of many of the leading lights of the design profession. Some of those individuals have been lost to the annals of history. Others are known to us and deserve our thanks.

Needfinding as a concept was originally pioneered by Robert McKim, the former head of the Design Division at Stanford University.

The introduction draws from material in "Needfinding: The Why and How of "Needfinding: The Why and How of Uncovering People's Needs" co-authored with Robert Becker.

The Design Process diagram was originally created by Charles Owens, a professor at the Illinois Institute of Technology. It has been modified significantly from its earlier version.

A.E.I.O.U. was originally developed by Rick Robinson, the founder of E*Lab.

Questions to Ask were originally developed by Michael Barry, a founder of Point Forward and a Consulting Professor at Stanford University.

Idea Logs were pioneered by numerous inventors and designers, most notably Leonardo daVinci. A page from his Codex Atlanticus f.386r Archimedes Screws and Water Wheels appears here.

Mindmaps and the examples included were originally developed by Rolf Faste, a previous head of the Product Design Program at Stanford University.

Visualizing Abstract Ideas is a drawing that was created by Dana Mauriello, a student and Product Design major at Stanford.

Powers of Ten is a concept that was originally presented in a film of the same name that was created by Charles and Ray Eames for IBM Corporation.

Frames and Frame Analysis draws from the work of Jerome Bruner, a cognitive psychologist and research fellow at the New York University School of Law.

The Out of Box Experience framework was developed by James L. Adams, a Professor Emeritus in the Design Division at Stanford University.

The Hierarchy of Needs was originally developed by American psychologist Abraham Maslow.

The Needs Hierarchy for Designers was created by me and was originally published in the Design Management Journal.

Pattern Languages draws on the work of Christopher Alexander, an architect and Professor Emeritus at the University of California, Berkeley.

Metaphors and how it appears in language draws from the work of George Lakoff, a cognitive linguist and Professor of Linguistics at the University of California, Berkeley.

The Ten Habits of Great Ideators was originally developed by Neal Moore and Dev Patnaik.

Marker Pad ideation was provided by Nike, Inc.

The cover design was created by Shilpa Sarkar.

Ami Rao oversaw the development and revision of the 4th edition.

Needfinding: Design Research and Planning

CPSIA information can be obtained
at www.ICGtesting.com
Printed in the USA
LVHW061503110922
728095LV00008B/620

9 781974 015580